AF378896

101 Ways to Score Higher on Your GMAT

What You Need to Know About the Graduate Management Admission Test Explained Simply

By Arlene Connolly

101 Ways to Score Higher on Your GMAT: What You Need to Know About the Graduate Management Admission Test Explained Simply

Copyright © 2008 by Atlantic Publishing Group, Inc.
1405 SW 6th Ave. • Ocala, Florida 34471 • 800-814-1132 • 352-622-1875–Fax
Web site: www.atlantic-pub.com • E-mail: sales@atlantic-pub.com
SAN Number: 268-1250

No part of this publication may be reproduced, stored in a retrieval system, or transmitted in any form or by any means, electronic, mechanical, photocopying, recording, scanning, or otherwise, except as permitted under Section 107 or 108 of the 1976 United States Copyright Act, without the prior written permission of the Publisher. Requests to the Publisher for permission should be sent to Atlantic Publishing Group, Inc., 1405 SW 6th Ave., Ocala, Florida 34471.

ISBN-13: 978-1-60138-252-8   ISBN-10: 1-60138-252-9

Library of Congress Cataloging-in-Publication Data

Connolly, Arlene, 1939-
  101 ways to score higher on your GMAT : what you need to know about the Graduate Management Admission Test explained simply / by Arlene Connolly.
      p. cm.
  Includes bibliographical references and index.
  ISBN-13: 978-1-60138-252-8 (alk. paper)
  ISBN-10: 1-60138-252-9 (alk. paper)
  1. Graduate Management Admission Test--Study guides. 2. Management--Examinations, questions, etc. 3. Business schools--United States--Entrance examinations--Study guides. 4. Universities and colleges--United States--Graduate work--Examinations--Study guides. I. Title. II. Title: One hundred and one ways to score higher on your GMAT.

  HF1118.C658 2008
  658.0076--dc22
                          2008023669

LIMIT OF LIABILITY/DISCLAIMER OF WARRANTY: The publisher and the author make no representations or warranties with respect to the accuracy or completeness of the contents of this work and specifically disclaim all warranties, including without limitation warranties of fitness for a particular purpose. No warranty may be created or extended by sales or promotional materials. The advice and strategies contained herein may not be suitable for every situation. This work is sold with the understanding that the publisher is not engaged in rendering legal, accounting, or other professional services. If professional assistance is required, the services of a competent professional should be sought. Neither the publisher nor the author shall be liable for damages arising herefrom. The fact that an organization or Web site is referred to in this work as a citation and/or a potential source of further information does not mean that the author or the publisher endorses the information the organization or Web site may provide or recommendations it may make. Further, readers should be aware that Internet Web sites listed in this work may have changed or disappeared between when this work was written and when it is read.

INTERIOR LAYOUT DESIGN: Nicole Deck ndeck@atlantic-pub.com

Printed in the United States

We recently lost our beloved pet "Bear," who was not only our best and dearest friend but also the "Vice President of Sunshine" here at Atlantic Publishing. He did not receive a salary but worked tirelessly 24 hours a day to please his parents. Bear was a rescue dog that turned around and showered myself, my wife Sherri, his grandparents Jean, Bob and Nancy and every person and animal he met (maybe not rabbits) with friendship and love. He made a lot of people smile every day.

We wanted you to know that a portion of the profits of this book will be donated to The Humane Society of the United States.

–Douglas & Sherri Brown

THE HUMANE SOCIETY
OF THE UNITED STATES ©

The human-animal bond is as old as human history. We cherish our animal companions for their unconditional affection and acceptance. We feel a thrill when we glimpse wild creatures in their natural habitat or in our own backyard.

Unfortunately, the human-animal bond has at times been weakened. Humans have exploited some animal species to the point of extinction.

The Humane Society of the United States makes a difference in the lives of animals here at home and worldwide. The HSUS is dedicated to creating a world where our relationship with animals is guided by compassion. We seek a truly humane society in which animals are respected for their intrinsic value, and where the human-animal bond is strong.

Want to help animals? We have plenty of suggestions. Adopt a pet from a local shelter, join The Humane Society and be a part of our work to help companion animals and wildlife. You will be funding our educational, legislative, investigative and outreach projects in the U.S. and across the globe.

Or perhaps you'd like to make a memorial donation in honor of a pet, friend or relative? You can through our Kindred Spirits program. And if you'd like to contribute in a more structured way, our Planned Giving Office has suggestions about estate planning, annuities, and even gifts of stock that avoid capital gains taxes.

Maybe you have land that you would like to preserve as a lasting habitat for wildlife. Our Wildlife Land Trust can help you. Perhaps the land you want to share is a backyard—that's enough. Our Urban Wildlife Sanctuary Program will show you how to create a habitat for your wild neighbors.

So you see, it's easy to help animals. And The HSUS is here to help.

The Humane Society of the United States
2100 L Street NW
Washington, DC 20037
202-452-1100
www.hsus.org

TABLE OF CONTENTS

INTRODUCTION

As you read this book, you may have an undergraduate degree in business administration and want to advance your career, you may be thinking about going back to school, or maybe you would like to change careers. In all three cases, going to business school to earn your Master of Business Administration (MBA) degree may be the step you need to take in order to increase your earning power and achieve success and satisfaction in your career. At the same time, it will also involve a significant investment of time and money, and you will need to plan and prepare carefully if you decide to take that step.

This book is intended to help you focus on your motives for going to graduate school and visualize what a career in management entails in today's world on various levels. It will also show you how to go about applying for admission and why finding the school that is right for you and financing your education in the right way are so important. In addition, it provides a picture of what graduate school will be like, whether you study on a full-time or part-time basis, attend classes here or abroad, or want to pursue an online MBA.

Special attention is given to the nature, importance, and scoring of the two standardized tests you will be required to take as part of your admission application — the Graduate Record

Examination (GRE) and the Graduate Management Admission Test (GMAT®). Valuable information is also provided about preparing for these exams and getting through both test days successfully. At the same time, you will be shown how to develop your job-hunting skills in a professional manner and use them throughout your career.

You will also discover that an MBA degree can be applied in many fields outside of the traditional corporate setting. The training and experience that are part of going through a business school curriculum can be directly applied to any of the following fields:

- Accounting and finance

- Advertising and marketing

- Business law

- Consulting

- E-commerce and entrepreneurship

- Healthcare

- Human resources

- Information technology

- Public administration

- Project management

- Risk management

Chapter 1
Why You Should Want to Get an MBA Degree

Most MBA students are between the ages of 25 and 34, but you are the sole judge of when it is the right time for you to accept the challenge of continuing your education. If you feel you have reached a plateau in your present job, a graduate degree may be just what you need to boost your career to the next level if you think you would be comfortable filling a management position.

Tip #1: Deciding if a Master's Degree Is What You Need to Help Your Career

As a manager, the most important skill you need to develop is your ability to interact with people, and this is accomplished by learning how they think, react, and function in a wide variety of circumstances. If you cultivate a genuine respect for your staff and are able to work with them as a team, you will have a positive effect on their behavior and will help them to become more productive on the job.

One of the reasons you may decide to seek a management position is that you want to increase your income, and you may also feel that such a position comes with a certain amount of authority and prestige. You will have authority as a manager, but you will also soon discover this power comes from the people you manage because they have trust in your leadership ability and are willing to follow. This is the only way in which a manager on any level can be effective.

Tip #2: Seeing if You Have the Potential to Be a Good Manager

While some aspects of filling a management position may appeal to you, you will need to engage in a certain amount of self-examination before you decide to proceed any further. Here are a few points to consider as you go through the process:

- You must be prepared to manage your career, which includes recognizing your dominant skills, abilities, and inclinations and applying them to whatever position you hold at work. Doing this also involves setting goals for yourself and making use of the opportunities for growth and advancement that present themselves throughout your career.

- You must be ready to continue your education, which will involve time, energy, and a financial commitment on your part. Finding exactly the right program is essential if you want to succeed.

- As a manager, you will need to cope with many different personalities and build an effective team with the staff you have to carry out your department's goals and be productive. In the end, you will be responsible to upper management for what those individuals do or fail to do.

Tip #3: Developing the Qualities a Good Manager Needs to Succeed

While you should have confidence in yourself and the skills you have developed, good managers also know there is always more for us to learn, and we are all works in progress. Good managers are comfortable when dealing with people, honest and open in their approach to them, and mindful that their success and the productivity of their department hinge on the trust their staff places in them. When a group project is planned, good managers make an effort to include everyone, and to do this, they try to become familiar with each person's capabilities and limitations.

Learn What Goes into Decision Making and Practice It Every Day

Although good managers are responsible for making decisions and living with the consequences, they are also aware that they need input from their staff, need to provide positive feedback to the group, and need to make good use of the information they receive if they are to decide correctly. Adopting this management style also contributes to building a genuine team spirit within the group, which is essential for good morale and high productivity level.

Tip #4: How to Show Your Boss That You Are a "Promotable" Employee

If you are in an entry-level or middle-management position

and want to advance your career, you can take certain strategic steps to convince your superiors that you are ready to move on to a higher position. If you practice these steps routinely, they will become second nature to you; in time, they will also have their desired effect.

1. **Make it obvious that you are prepared to move up the career ladder**. Do your present job efficiently and professionally, show that you are ready to take on additional work, and make every effort to maintain good rapport with upper-level management. To establish and maintain your credibility with others, never "play favorites" with your employees, keep any promises you make, unless unexpected events make that impossible (which will require an explanation on your part), and make every effort to remain neutral when a dispute arises.

2. **Show your boss that you have the self-confidence a manager needs**. If you take some practical steps to develop this character trait that is so essential in earning a promotion, you will find this will then become obvious to others. Here are a few suggestions for you to follow:

    • **Try to learn from your past mistakes**. Besides telling yourself that you do not want to repeat them again, use them as genuine learning experiences. For example, if your basic idea was sound in a project you attempted, determine whether you should have allotted more time to complete it, requested additional resources, or hired more workers.

    • **Focus your attention on what needs to be done**

rather than on yourself. If you are scheduled to give a presentation, for example, make sure the two most important factors are your audience and the message you want to convey to them. Once you learn to do this, you will find that the matter of self-confidence is no longer much of an issue.

- **Emulate what you admire in others who appear self-assured.** You will soon conclude that they appear calm, make eye contact, carry themselves well, and have a convincing smile. In addition, while it is not as obvious as those external characteristics, you can be certain that these individuals have learned to think positively as well. Deep-breathing exercises, meditation or yoga, repeating an appropriate mantra, or picturing a peaceful scene may all prove helpful here.

- **Appreciate your successes, both large and small.** They are signs that your work has value, that others benefit from and appreciate it, that you possess unique skills and abilities, and that others have placed confidence in you in the past and were not disappointed.

3. **Try to act as a link between upper management and your staff**. While part of your job involves carrying out established organizational procedures and providing information to your employees, you should also be ready to act as an advocate for them and be ready to bring their complaints, concerns, and requests to upper management. By doing this, you will build up the trust and confidence both groups have in you and acquire a reputation as a

problem solver at the same time. In addition, bringing out the potential of those you supervise and helping them to become more productive will indicate that you have the qualities of a true leader.

4. **Keep up with the latest developments in your organization and your industry**. Subscribing to at least one professional journal should help you do this and will enable you to present your creative ideas to the "top brass" for their consideration, answer your employees' questions effectively, and highlight your credibility at the same time. Note that if you become involved in a company project that is not directly related to your position, your interest in it must be genuine. Being noticed for what you are doing should be only a side issue here, not the motivating factor. In this way, upper management will know that you are versatile, flexible, and willing to take on new challenges.

5. **Be ready to seek advice from others as you advance in your career**. Make an effort to establish relationships with people who are truly successful, either within your organization or elsewhere in your industry. As mentors with good judgment and considerable experience, they can provide you with the advice and encouragement you need to advance in your career, and they will appreciate the confidence you place in them.

You will feel the need for a mentor most acutely when certain critical situations crop up on the job, such as:

- **You are finding it difficult to get along with your boss**. When this has been going on for a long time, you will want to improve the situation, transfer to another department, or look for another job. Being objective, your mentor can help you determine if the problem is caused by poor communication between you and your boss, a personality clash, or some other factor, and you will find it easier to work out a solution on that basis.

- **You have been trying to earn a promotion without success**. It has not been forthcoming, even though your performance reviews have been positive for many years, and you feel that you are "marching in place" and have to be proactive at this point. If your mentor works for your company, the two of you can determine what the stumbling blocks to your advancement are and decide exactly how you can work around them to advance your career.

- **You have been assigned a task that seems both challenging and formidable**. Since a mentor in the business world fills a role that is similar to a coach working with a sports team, this person will help you assess your skills, anticipate the problems, and take preventive measures as you carry out your assignment. Such help is often based on personal experience.

Tip #5: Some Subtle Steps You Can Take to Advance Your Career

Those who work in marketing and advertising are well aware of the effect a "subliminal message" can have, and there are certain habits you can cultivate to convince others that you would be able to handle extra responsibilities on the job with ease and deserve a promotion. Here are just a few of them for you to consider:

- **Make yourself a known quantity in your organization**. Whenever you have something worthwhile to say in the course of a business discussion, do not hesitate to join in. This will indicate that you are interested and enthusiastic about your organization or the project you have undertaken. Also, when a meeting is scheduled, go over the agenda and prepare your comments to achieve a similar effect. In addition, taking a seat near the person conducting the meeting will make it easier for you to be seen and heard, will prompt you to participate more fully, and will serve as a sign of your support.

- **Be willing to do more than is expected of you**. Without being heavy handed in any way, help your coworkers with their assignments or be willing to do something that is not part of your job description. Note that if you exercise tact in doing this, you will likely relieve your superiors of some of the angst related to delegating assignments, and it will not go unnoticed. Also, when you receive compliments from someone for doing a good job, accept them graciously, but never accept credit that belongs to someone else or that should be shared with others.

- **Your casual conversations also tell people something about you**. They will soon discover if you are open to suggestions, willing to share ideas, criticize others when they are out of earshot, and can keep confidences. Note also that a bit of socializing helps to build rapport with your colleagues and fosters the team spirit so highly prized by upper management.

- **Always take the time to thank others for what they have done**. Your gratitude must be sincere, and you do not have to "gush" in order to get your message across. In addition, this will show your respect and kindness for the other person, who will likely be more than willing to come to your assistance in the future as a result.

Tip #6: Learn How to Function as an Effective Leader

In order to exercise genuine leadership as a manager and advance your career, you must keep the following points in mind:

- **Your first job is to keep your team on track**. Regardless of how many people you supervise, your first priority should be focusing on the main goal the group is meant to accomplish. This will enable you to stop from time to time, assess how far you have come in reaching that objective, and determine what still needs to be done. If, at any time, you see that little or no progress has been made, you will have to alter your current strategy in order to close the gap and reach your goal at the designated time.

- **Never forget that you are also a work in progress**. There is always more for you to learn. You should use every opportunity that presents itself for sharpening your skills. This spirit is catching, and it is quite possible that your team will follow your example.

- **Your personal integrity is your most valuable asset**. Keeping the goals of your group in mind will help you avoid being self-indulgent or becoming power-happy, and you will earn the respect of those you supervise at the same time.

- **Always take good care of your team (staff) and look out for their welfare**. Be aware of the things the people on your team need to do their job, and make every effort to provide it for them. Make it clear to your staff that they can always come to you with any problems or concerns they may have.

- **Use your authority wisely and avoid any sign of arrogance**. Responsibilities come with every management position, along with certain "perks" and a substantial salary. Following the previous steps will help you to carry out those responsibilities like a true leader.

Tip #7: Learn to Work with Many Different Personality Types

As a manager, you will often have to deal with various personality types, including difficult people, whether they intend to be that way. To do that effectively, you will need to determine what they are like and react appropriately in order to maintain departmental morale or defuse a volatile situation. In addition, these individuals tend to fall into one of these main categories:

- **Those who are sometimes openly aggressive**. These people are often irrational when they become angry, and it is best to let them have their say before you respond. Then, express your views confidently and calmly to show that you have not been intimidated by them.

- **Those who are often "too quiet."** People in this category may sometimes make you feel that you do not exist by ignoring you, creating an undercurrent of tension, and responding to your attempts at conversation with monosyllables. Learn to be patient with such people, ask them questions that require more than "yes" or "no" for an answer, and listen carefully when they finally respond.

- **Those who are always negative**. This group can drag down the morale of your entire staff, and while you may sympathize with the unfortunate things that have happened to them and made them that way, your main objective will be to offset their negativity, and perhaps brighten their outlook, by setting a positive, upbeat tone in the office.

- **Those who are sullen**. These individuals are more complex than those who are openly aggressive, and they attempt to cover their hostility with humor, are often sarcastic, and show disapproval by their facial expressions and gestures. Since they also are often rather cowardly, you may find that their behavior changes quickly once you confront them about it.

Avoid taking the words and actions of difficult people personally, as hard as that might be at times, since they are often the result of bad habits these people have developed over time. If you are consistent in dealing with them on a day-to-day basis, your frustration level will decrease and you will be able to do your job more effectively.

Tip #8: Learn How to Hire the Right People for Your Team

When you have a job slot to fill, you will want to find the ideal candidate in the most efficient way possible, rather than simply resorting to the "help wanted" pages of your local newspaper. Here are some additional steps you can take:

- **Subscribe to one or more professional e-mail lists in the employer category**. Doing this will enable you to choose from a database of applicants who are seeking employment in your industry, and it will also serve as a screening device. You might find these Web sites helpful: **www.lists.com** and **http://e-news-letters.internet.com/mailinglists.html**.

- **Determine if any of the reliable independent contractors (freelancers) who work for your company are interested in becoming full-time employees**. To some extent, such an individual is already a known quantity, and if you meet to discuss the possibility of making this change, you may be able to work out the details to your mutual satisfaction and fill the job opening with ease.

- **Make good use of the employees you already have working for you**. Do not hesitate to post job openings within your organization, because someone on the staff may have the qualifications you require, even if they are working in another capacity, such as administrative support. Orientation for such an individual would be simplified, because he or she will already be familiar with your company's policies and procedures.

Tip #9: What You Can Do When You Supervise a Large Staff

If you have the task of supervising many employees and have learned to delegate well, there is a danger that you may become too comfortable with the status quo and start taking your staff for granted. Regardless of how busy you are, you should never become so preoccupied that you fail to monitor what is going on from day to day. In addition, if your company or department is growing rapidly, be aware that this will prove to be a special challenge in your situation.

Here are a few steps you can take when you find yourself facing this situation:

- **Be sure that you have an established performance appraisal system in place**. Taking this step will help you keep things in perspective and treat your employees fairly, and you may also decide that self-appraisals and peer review should be a part of the process.

- **Check to see if the right person is doing the right job**. Authorities on management refer to this as "division of labor," and it entails assigning a particular task to the individual who is best-suited to it. This is also considered a win-win situation because your employees will be more productive and content, and you will able to meet your deadlines for completing projects more easily.

- **Provide the people on your staff with the training they need**. This will help boost their morale and productivity, enable them to do what you are asking of them, and aid in maintaining an effective team. With this in mind, try to create an environment where mutual trust and respect are the norm and the ethical standards are high. The possibility for conflict is greater in a larger group, and you will want to sharpen your negotiating skills and use them when the need arises.

Tip #10: Master the Art of Being a Good Listener When Dealing with Others

Here are some subtle techniques, which, when taken together, will help you develop your listening skills and become an effective, much-appreciated communicator on all levels:

- If someone comes to you with a complaint or problem,

for example, try paraphrasing what the other person is saying from time to time for the sake of clarification and to show that you are giving him or her your complete attention. In addition, neither of you should be permitted to dominate the conversation, because it should be a process of give-and-take.

- Maintaining confidentiality at all times is essential if you want to experience the trust and cooperation of your staff. When you are dealing with a third party and feel the need to share a specific incident, only do so if you can accomplish it without getting into the details of the case or mentioning any names.

Try to be totally open to what the other person is telling you. There is an old saying that "even a broken clock is right twice a day," and this individual may be able to shed new light on a topic, as unlikely as that may seem. This can even be true when you are dealing with a subject that stirs up strong emotions within you, such as the departmental budget. It also means that you should never attempt to formulate an answer in your mind until you have absorbed all of the information being provided and the time is appropriate for you to respond.

- If you are working under a tight deadline or some other stress factor that is preventing you from giving the other person your full attention or is keeping you from providing a response, arrange to take up the issue again soon at a more convenient time, or indicate when an answer will be forthcoming. By doing this, you will provide assurance that, one way or another, the matter under discussion will get the attention it deserves.

Tip #11: Learn the Importance of Ethics in Any Manager's Life

Dictionary.com defines ethics as "the rules of conduct recognized in respect to a particular class of human actions or a particular group, culture, etc.: medical ethics; Christian ethics." This tells us that the business world should also be guided by the core principles that determine its code of conduct, and this is especially true when managers and their staff discover that the organization is going to downsize or is going out of business altogether.

According to federal law, a company with more than 100 employees must give at least 60 days' notice before ceasing operation or laying off 50 or more full-time employees. This measure is intended to shorten the time when these individuals will be between jobs, which means that they will need to collect less unemployment as a result.

In addition, the company should also tell their shareholders that they intend to take such action, because this will help shareholders determine if they want to reduce the number of shares they will keep or sell all of them. Also, every organization doing business with this company, including your suppliers, should be informed of this decision so they can plan accordingly.

Tip #12: Never Overlook the Importance of Planning in a Manager's Life

As a manager, one of your goals will be to become an expert planner, whether that involves lining up today's to-do list for yourself or setting goals for the company's next fiscal year. Being expert planner means thinking about the future and what it may hold for business as a whole and your company in particular. You will also be proactive in facing the problems and changes that will inevitably occur, rather than engaging in the catch-up exercise known as "damage control." Your aim is to control events as much as possible, rather than having them control you.

Along with your planning skill, you should develop an entrepreneurial attitude that helps you determine new and better ways of doing things. Since you do not want to settle for the status quo, you should constantly search for opportunities that will lead to improvement and know how to make use of them when they occur.

Tip #13: Some Dangers You Will Want to Avoid as a Manager

Whether you are an entry-level manager or advancing in your career, certain negative factors can creep into your workday almost imperceptibly. They may undermine your success as a manager as you try to fulfill the various responsibilities that are part of your job description and complete the many projects assigned to you. Here is what you should look for and guard against in that situation:

- **Try not to become too isolated from other people on the job**. Get to know the organization or department that you supervise by making yourself known and being approachable, rather than merely relying on the formal reports and summaries that are submitted to you. You need both in order to know what is going on, what action should be taken, and how to plan for the future.

- **Be open to suggestions and recommendations from others**. (1) Decisions should not be made in haste, (2) you can always learn from the insights and observations of others, and (3) they should know that you are always ready to listen to them and respect what they have to say.

- **Be unwilling to keep anyone on your staff who has a proven record of mediocre job performance**. If you do, your failure to remedy the situation will reflect on your ability as a leader and the productivity of the group will suffer as well. In order to be fair, you should also be willing to give this employee a reasonable time limit to improve, depending on the seriousness of the situation.

- **Try to plan carefully and keep your priorities in order**. If you show that you can stay focused on the goals you have set for your company or department rather than constantly coming up with a new "project du jour" that takes your staff by surprise or setting unrealistic expectations for the group, they will appreciate the effort you have made and will follow your example.

Tip #14: Learn the Importance of Time Management in a Manager's Life

Good time management is essential for anyone completing a

graduate program or pursuing a career in business. You can learn to make good use of your time by following these simple steps:

- **Begin by taking a look at what you do with your time.** Time is a precious commodity, and it is certainly not something we would knowingly waste, but if you ever find yourself asking, "Where did the time go?" you might want to keep track of how you spend your time for a week or so in order to answer that question. Use the form that seems most practical to you in order to do this, and determine if constant interruptions aren't part of the problem. Only then will you know how to improve the situation.

- **Determine what changes you need to make to use time more effectively.** Once you have done your tracking, it may be obvious that you need to do less "starting and stopping" during the day. If you develop the habit of making several phone calls at a set time instead of spacing them out, for example, or get into the habit of checking and responding to your e-mail when you first arrive at the office (and perhaps after lunch), you will be surprised at how much you can accomplish in the course of the day.

- **Time management tools can also help.** If you have a software calendar or some Day-Timer® product to keep track of your schedule and upcoming events, you will feel more in control of your time than if you simply trust to memory.

- **Start the day off the right way to set the right tone.**

Begin by thinking about the tasks you have lined up for the day and then list them in order of importance so that you will know where to start. This will also be a sign to your staff that you have your goals in mind and your priorities in order. In other words, there is something to be said for having an established routine. In addition, you will be able to save precious time every day if your files and records are kept in good order.

- **Be aware that micromanaging is a dangerous thing to do**. As a manager, you will be busy interacting with other people in management, overseeing projects, troubleshooting, monitoring production, and developing or maintaining relationships with customers. If you become bogged down in minutiae and make the mistake of micromanaging your staff, you will lose sight of the big picture and fail to reach the goals you originally established for yourself.

Here are some hints to keep you from falling into the micromanaging trap, which can eventually cause you to suffer "burnout" and create discontent and low morale within your staff:

1. **Do not forget that there is more than one way to do a job well**. Let your employees know the results you expect from their work and when it should be completed, and then let them proceed in their own way. Keep the lines of communication open to see how things are going and answer any questions they may have, but avoid treating them like children. You want them to function as a team and be productive in a positive atmosphere.

2. **Have mutual trust as a top priority**. As a leader, you will want your employees to trust and respect you, and this should always be reciprocated. Unfortunately, if you attempt to micromanage everything they do, your employees' sense of responsibility and decision-making skills will deteriorate, along with the morale in your department. At the same time, providing your staff with the necessary training and setting an example for them to follow should eliminate any perceived need for micromanaging on your part.

3. **Do not be afraid to delegate work to your staff when you can**. Delegating work is often a necessity for any manager and a skill that he or she should acquire, but it is also something that should never be done on a hit-or-miss basis. In addition, you should not delegate any project that is confidential in nature or that your boss clearly indicated should only be done by you. You will gain the cooperation of your staff if they are given something that is enjoyable or interesting to do from time to time, along with the many nuts-and-bolts type of assignments that come along.

Tip #15: Delegating the Right Way Is Always Essential

Here are some factors to consider when exercising the option of delegating work to your staff to ensure that the results will be satisfactory:

- **Be sure to pick the right person to complete the job**. Your choice should be based on an individual's skills, productivity, and motivation, along with the realization that most of us enjoy a challenge from time to time and often rise to the occasion when we are presented with one. Be prepared to exercise patience until the task is complete.

- **Explain what needs to be done to the person who is assigned the project**. If you ask an employee to perform an unfamiliar task, be sure to supply clear instructions, and put them in writing if they are lengthy or complex in order to avoid confusion and disappointing results. When people show you that they are equal to the task, you can take this as indication that they are ready to play a greater role in the decision-making process.

- **Monitor the progress of the work you assign**. Let your employees know how accountable they will be and how their performance will be measured whenever you delegate. If a project is large enough to warrant it, you can divide it into smaller segments. Assign these segments to several people and stipulate that they should report back to you when a particular segment is complete. You will also gain valuable feedback from them through the staff meetings you schedule and the special reports they submit to you, and they will know that you are well aware of everything that is being done in your department.

If you master the art of delegating, your employees will also benefit from it. They will always have the feeling that they can come to you with any questions, that they can learn from their mistakes, that they will be commended when they have done a good job, and that you will never take credit for any accomplishment that was theirs.

Tip #16: Learn to Be Cautious When It Comes to Multitasking

Some people feel that multitasking is the key to managing their time effectively, but when we consider that the term was originally used to define "the concurrent performance of several jobs by a computer," we can see that there is danger in its overuse by humans, since we are not machines and should never attempt to function the way they do. Here are some cautions for you to consider:

- **Be aware that multitasking can become addictive, even when it fails to increase your productivity.** Here are some things you can do to reduce the need for multitasking in your life and lower your daily stress level at the same time:

1. Avoid endless paper shuffling in the office by handling every hardcopy business document as soon as you receive it. In almost every case, you will need to respond to it, act on its recommendations, or see that it is filed properly for future reference.

2. Instant messaging can be helpful in communicating with others if you use it sparingly. Treat everyone courteously by avoiding interruptions from your cell phone or pager when you meet with them.

3. Try to determine the length of time it will take to complete

the tasks on your "to do" list when you review it, and then see how close your estimate comes to being accurate. This will enable you to monitor your interruptions, keep your priorities in order, and decide when you need to delegate a particular task to someone on your staff.

- **Multitasking can also be harmful**. The most extreme example that comes to mind is the individual who attempts to drive and talk on the cell phone at the same time. The danger increases with the complexity of the mental tasks we are attempting to perform. As the tension mounts in such a situation, people become less efficient at what they are doing, and, over time, they also experience a decrease in job satisfaction. In addition, researchers have found that when multitasking is overdone, we can experience short-term memory loss, depression, anxiety, and mental burnout.

- **Technology is not the villain here**. We need to respond to its influence in the right way, and if we fail to do so, we will become virtual slaves to technology instead of using it to enhance our lives and the lives of others. To gain the upper hand here, we need to adjust to its speed and the realization that it can be found virtually everywhere, and avoid becoming overly dependent on a vast array of electronic gadgets.

Conclusion

If you feel that getting an MBA will help you advance in the job market and you have the potential to succeed as a manager, you will want to proceed carefully to reach your goal. Here are some things you can do throughout your career in order to succeed:

- Develop your leadership, planning, and time management skills.

- Learn how to work with various personality types and become a good listener.

- Make an effort to hire the right people for your department.

- Delegate work whenever that becomes necessary and avoid micromanaging.

- Be cautious about multitasking.

Chapter 2
Deciding if You Want to be a Manager

Since enrolling in an MBA program involves a considerable commitment on your part, and even though you may be aware of the advantages that come with a management position, you should never take that step on a whim or before weighing all the factors involved. The information that follows will help you to do just that.

Tip #17: Consider the Negative Side of Being in a Management Position

While you want to establish a good relationship with everyone you supervise and promote a team spirit within the group as a manager, you will also need to be a little removed from your staff so that you can be objective in making the difficult decisions — for which you will be held accountable by your superiors — that are often part of a manager's job description.

Here are some other points that you will need to think about if you want to assume the role of manager or advance your career:

- The goals of your department will often be long-term, sometimes quarterly or annual in scope, and it will be up to you to keep your employees' morale up, as well as your own, until those goals are realized or adjusted to meet current needs.

- At every management level, you will find at least one person who is intent on replacing you, feels that he or she could do a better job, and may even be trying to take your job. There may not be a personal element in such a situation at all; it simply goes with the territory and is a sign of that individual's innate competitiveness and ambition.

- Occasionally, you will have to take a position that your staff will neither like nor understand because your main priority will be your organization's main goals, objectives, and mission, and you never want to lose sight of that.

Tip #18: Decide if You Need a Career Change

If you want to make a total career change or take steps to advance your career in the field you are already in, you will want to plan carefully in making such a move. Taking the time to think about what you must do is essential in order to avoid serious missteps or landing in a job that is far different from what you thought it would be. Here are some suggestions for you to follow as you make your decision:

- **Be sure that you move at the right time for the right reason.** Consider the overall condition of the job market in your area at the time, and make sure that such a drastic move is necessary to get rid of your dissatisfaction. If you are uncomfortable in the culture of your company or tired of a lengthy commute, this does not mean you need to switch to an entirely new industry to resolve the situation.

- **Find out exactly what you will be getting into if you change careers.** This is the time to do some networking, gather information about the field that interests you from reliable resources on the Internet, and consult with a career counselor as you make your decision. This is not the time to rush into anything; no deadline will be hanging over your head, and you might not be able to match your current salary when you first change careers. There is a reason for the saying, "Be careful what you wish for, you might get it."

- **If you decide to consult a career counselor, choose the right one.** To accomplish this, work with an experienced adviser with one or more college degrees. In addition, to ensure that you will be given accurate information, this individual should be certified by National Certification Corporation (NCC) or River Parishes Community College (RPCC), or as a psychologist and specialize in the field that interests you.

- **Determine why you want to make such a change.** Along with thinking about what you dislike in your present position, consider what you expect to find in your new job and what you want to bring to it. While you may want to increase your income by making such a move, you will also want to feel a certain sense of accomplishment in your new career, and you may also need to acquire additional credentials, such as an MBA, in order to reach your goal.

- **Bring your job-hunting skills up to date.** If several years have passed since your last job interview, you may be surprised at how out-of-practice you feel. Do some practice interviewing with a friend or family member, and learn how to look for a job on the Internet. In addition, be certain that your résumé is up to date and geared to the new field you have chosen.

- **Getting an MBA can prepare you for future career hurdles in business.** In the course of your career, you will experience rapid and constant change, both in your employment and in moving into various fields of knowledge as the needs of the business world change; you will need to adapt to this change to succeed. Earning your business degree will prepare you for this necessary adjustment and arm you with the training you will need to enjoy going to work every day throughout your career.

- **Proceed with caution as you take this step.** While earning a graduate degree can certainly help advance your career and increase your income, there is no easy formula for getting from where you are now to where you want to be. Here are a few things for you to think about:

1. **Do not consider your current job irrelevant when looking for a new one.** Today, being bilingual is a definite advantage

in the marketplace, and it is sometimes said that "versatility equals employability." This means that once you have your MBA, your varied training, work experience, and multiple skills will work to your advantage.

2. **Realize that you may have to take a cut in salary at first.** If you are making a career change and have been making a good salary, be aware that you will be an entry-level job candidate in a certain sense when you first receive your MBA. In this situation, completing an internship related to your graduate program may be especially helpful, because you will gain practical experience related to business school and establish new contacts that may lead to a job offer.

Tip #19: Why Getting Your MBA Can Increase Your Career Options and Your Yearly Income

While some business school graduates work for large organizations with structured career paths where long hours are the norm, once you have your advanced degree, it will be possible for you to do something completely different. In reality, getting your MBA can help you balance the demands of career and family because of its flexibility.

What follows are just some of the career options that will be available to you when you earn you degree, depending on the exact course of study you complete in business school and your individual career goals:

1. **Accounting and management.** The accountant's goal is to provide reliable, pertinent information to investors, managers, government, and creditors, along with the

general public. In the business world, this data is used in making investment decisions, dispensing credit, and maintaining the fiscal integrity of an organization by monitoring its "bottom line."

Most employers will consider it a "bonus" if you are a Certified Public Accountant (CPA) with an MBA degree, which will enable you to negotiate a higher salary when you interview for a job. In addition, getting your business degree will help you enhance the skills you have already developed through your business and academic experience. The University of Chicago's Graduate School of Business, one of the nation's top business schools, with a quantitative and analytical focus in its course of study, places about 80 percent of its graduates in financial and consulting positions.

2. **Advertising and management.** This particular specialty is closely associated with business, and it is mainly used to communicate a particular message to a specific, targeted audience at a designated time. Those individuals who are responsible for organizing advertising campaigns are often trained in business practices that track current trends through their research and ensure that those campaigns will be effective at the same time.

If you choose to go into this field, your time will be divided between managing a creative advertising team and analyzing consumer behavior. With this in mind, your course of study should include these topics: research and statistics, law and ethics, brand management, and consumer behavior.

3. **Banking and finance management.** Since there are several types of banks — commercial banks, credit unions,

savings and loans, and federal reserves — a wide range of management positions are available for individuals who have business experience and an MBA degree, including insurance and financial risk management.

If you decide to specialize in this field of study, you will be able to apply the fundamentals of fund acquisition and portfolio management skills on a daily basis. You will be involved in completing audits, financial planning, dealing with tax laws, analyzing budgets, and working within the IT field. In addition, if you choose to become a financial consultant instead of working for an employer, you will be prepared to assist your clients with their investing, budgeting, and money management concerns.

To help you prepare for these financial positions, in your coursework, you will learn how to file income tax returns, work with various databases, and advise your customers on how to manage their assets. You will study financial risk management, fixed-income analysis, portfolio management and security analysis, and real estate and urban land economics. Some outstanding schools, including the Yale School of Management and Columbia Business School, provide excellent training in this area.

4. **Business administration and management.** MBAs who want to follow this career path will need to develop their expertise in running a successful organization and dealing with clients, stock holders, and employees at the same time. Understandably, this is the area of concentration most people associate with the training students receive when they attend business school to earn a graduate degree. Indeed, many of those who apply have already taken some

related courses or have majored in business administration on the undergraduate level.

If this is the type of program that interests you, the Tuck School of Business at Dartmouth, which specializes in this area along with many others, is a close-knit community that offers its students the unique combination of small class size and a challenging curriculum.

5. **Business law and management.** Some business lawyers deal with lawsuits, and they are known as *business litigators*¬. Others, who are referred to as *transactional lawyers*, deal with contracts and other corporate matters, including patents and bargaining agreements with labor unions. Acquiring an MBA degree adds to their effectiveness in the business world or at a governmental agency. In addition, having an onsite conflict manager to take the lead in resolving legal problems can save an organization negative publicity and costly litigation, which are always to be avoided.

Getting an MBA degree in conflict management and negotiation, for example, will provide you with a specialty that is essential today, when global, conflict-free commerce is the goal for companies doing business abroad. Such a program will concentrate on ethical negotiating skills, the various ways of coping with uncooperative negotiation participants, strategic planning, and international business relations.

In addition, a good program in this area will include courses related to negotiation theory and its practical application in the modern world. As a rule, it will include topics like research methods in conflict management, dispute methodology, assessing and understanding conflicts, third-party law, negotiation theory and practice, mediation theory and practice, arbitration theory and practice, and the origins of conflict.

6. **E-commerce and management.** As a business student, you will have some classes related to this topic in graduate school, but you may decide to specialize in this area because the related technology is expanding rapidly, the Internet is a powerful sales and marketing tool, and we are now living in a global economy. If you specialize in this area, you can expect to be involved in sales and marketing activity online, and you will need to have an understanding of Internet security issues to protect your employer and your clients from economic danger.

If you choose this as your specialty, your courses may cover topics like digital marketing, Internet business models, Web design, database management, project management, electronic security, supply chain management, information systems, and other issues related to organizations with an online presence.

7. **The global economy and management.** Since we live in a worldwide economy today, many American companies interact with foreign companies, their employees, and foreign agencies on a regular basis to conduct business profitably and professionally. Getting an MBA in global management will prepare you to meet the many multiethnic and multicultural challenges that such a position entails because of the knowledge, skills, and self-confidence you will acquire as you go through your graduate program.

In this kind of program, you will learn how the policies and laws governing the actions of different nations affect each other and how specific regions work together for their mutual benefit. You may be required to have knowledge of a second language and previous work experience abroad. In addition, your courses may include demography, comparative market systems, ethnic and race relations, diplomatic strategy, international politics, international business, global ecology, global trade and finance, theories of international relations, public international law, world history, and United States foreign policy.

8. **Healthcare administration.** If you choose this as your specialty, along with developing your business and management skills, you will be able to further your understanding of health maintenance and the treatment of disease. With this in mind, you should be prepared to take courses in patient communications, epidemiology, healthcare law, and other related topics, depending on the program you select.

For those who are interested in pursuing a career in healthcare administration, here is some detailed information that should help you in planning your graduate program and determining the kind of preparation you will need:

- **What you will be trained to do in business school.** Earning an MBA in healthcare administration can prepare you for a career as a healthcare manager, medical facility administrator, long-term care facility administrator, health insurance supervisor, medical claims manger, and other related positions.

- **What your graduate program will be like.** The essential courses in this kind of graduate program include healthcare administration, health facilities administration, patient management, medical terminology, health maintenance organization (HMO) processing, crisis intervention and management, conflict negotiation, information technology (IT) for health administration, medical ethics, medical research methods, and grant funding. You will also enhance your skills in human resource management and media relations as part of your program.

9. **Human resources (HR) department management.** Since virtually every employer with 50 or more people on their staff has an HR department, many jobs are available in this area. If you choose this as your specialty, you may become involved in recruiting and interviewing job applicants, carrying out corporate policy, and providing information related to employee assistance, benefits, and compensation. Also, if you train personnel by making presentations and conducting workshops for them, you will help them become more productive, enhance their skills, and increase their job satisfaction.

In the HR environment, the department staff and management need to be organized and thorough, and while working in this field can be interesting and rewarding, it can also be quite challenging and hectic at times. This explains why earning an MBA with this specialty may be essential if you are interested in a career in human resource management. In addition, managers in this field are expected to act as a liaison between the company's upper management and the employees, with the mission of maintaining a smooth operation, solving problems, and settling disputes. Occasionally, you may also become involved in helping to formulate policy and engage in strategic planning for your organization.

To do well in this field, you will need to possess outstanding "people skills," including the ability to cope with conflict, and practice fairness and discretion in dealing with others. You should also be skilled in the art of persuasion, sometimes known as the ability to "disagree without being disagreeable." You must be ready to work long hours when a major dispute arises, and some HR positions will require you to travel extensively, meaning that you will spend some time away from home.

10. **Information technology and management.** Specializing in this area means that you will gain a thorough knowledge of computer technology and its relationship to modern business procedures. As a result, your graduate courses will help you develop your expertise as a technician and prepare you to take on the role of business administrator at the same time.

If you decide to specialize in this area, your coursework may include topics such as enterprise systems and infrastructure, project management, and relevant electronic procedures based on a company's productivity and profitability. Also, the relatively new corporate title of Chief Information Officer (CIO) is used to designate the upper-level executive who is charged with overseeing the computer systems and information technology that carry out the company's mission.

If you have an interest in information technology and management, note that the MIT Sloan School of Management, the Haas School of Business at the University of California (Berkeley), and the McCombs School of Business at the University of Texas (Austin) are widely recognized for the training they provide in this area, and their programs may be of particular interest to you.

11. **Marketing and management.** If you specialize in this area, you will learn to understand why consumers behave in a certain way, to conduct effective advertising campaigns for your employer, and to interact professionally with companies and consumers alike. In addition, you will be prepared to fill positions in advertising, public relations, and corporate management as you go through your graduate program.

12. **Management jobs in the nonprofit sector.** The needs of a nonprofit organization in regard to management are similar to those of the for-profit business sector, but you will also be involved in activities that are unique to this type of operation. These ventures may include recruiting and retaining donors, informing the general public about your organization and its purpose, interacting with politicians and celebrities on behalf of your organization, organizing fundraisers, and engaging in widespread networking to carry out your organization's mission.

Today, many colleges and universities in the United States offer a variety of related programs, and since the need for capable managers in the nonprofit sector is large, this trend is likely to continue. If the thought of working in this area interests you, you should begin your program sooner rather than later because of the intense competition that exists currently.

If you decide to go this route, you will be able to choose from a variety of unique programs, including the Social Enterprise area of concentration that is offered by the Kellogg School of Business at Northwestern University. Also, Net Impact has published a survey, entitled *Business as Unusual*, focusing on about 40 business schools that provide socially aware courses of study.

While the salaries at nonprofit organizations may not equal those found in other business areas, having an advanced degree in management will give you a definite advantage, and it is not uncommon for a top nonprofit executive to earn $100,000 a year or more.

13. **Public administration and management.** People who specialize in this type of management are mainly involved in the operations of various government organizations and agencies throughout America. In addition, their special task is to meet the constantly changing needs of the citizens they serve, to communicate effectively with those on their staff, and to use the relatively limited amount of funds at their disposal in an ethical manner for the good of the people they serve on the local, state, or federal level.

14. **Risk management.** If you decide to specialize in this area, which is a fairly new and growing field, you will receive training and develop the preventive skills required to ensure that your company's future will be stable, which is what employers expect from their risk managers. The curriculum you follow will include topics such as environmental issues, general and legal insurance, and property estimation.

When you choose risk management, in your business school courses, you will become acquainted with current labor law, with emphasis on employee rights and benefits; casualty and health insurance; underwriting; and business liabilities, and you will be provided with the tools needed to prevent and reduce risk for your company in some capacity.

Tip #20: Some Job-hunting Strategies You Can Use Throughout Your Career

If you are going to make the commitment of time, energy, and talent that earning an MBA degree entails, you will want to sharpen your job-hunting skills to advance your career and increase your income. Here are some tips that should prove helpful as you set out to find a suitable management position, advance your career, and whenever you are looking for employment:

- **Make good use of all your networking opportunities.** The various relationships you will establish with your fellow students and the network you will form while you are earning your MBA are considered a significant and valuable part of the business school experience. Networking will also prove to be an incredible resource that you will appreciate and benefit from long after you have earned your degree.

In addition, authorities tell us that 75 percent or more of current job openings go unadvertised, and they are often filled by "word of mouth" (another term for networking) and promoting from within an organization, which is also the result of person-to-person communication.

- **Use your business school's career placement service when you are job hunting.** When you enroll for your graduate courses, you will be given information about any career placement services available to you as a student. This is a sign that your school is actively connected with various businesses, and you may discover that they also conduct job fairs periodically.

- **Register with reputable executive recruitment agencies and headhunters.** Once these organizations have the information they need about you as a job seeker, they will act as intermediaries as they try to find a job for you that matches the potential employer's specifications with your qualifications and salary requirements. A reputable job site in this category will use your profile to ensure human resource personnel that you are prequalified for the positions they have open at the time.

Tip #21: Why You Should Belong to a Professional Organization

While having an opportunity to do some networking and learn more about your chosen field could be a key reason for taking this step, such societies often have their own scholarship programs for their members. While you can learn more about them from their official publications and Web sites, here are some points to consider:

- **How you will benefit from joining such a group.** As a member, you may be entitled to free publications or receive a discount on certain books, journals, or magazines. This will enable you to keep up with recent developments in your chosen field or provide information that you can use when working on class assignments. In addition, their Web sites might enable you to link to their members-only job boards and message boards, which will also be helpful to you.

- **Why you should want to become an active member of a professional organization.** If the organization you join has a chapter on campus at your business school, you may find that they sponsor social, service, and educational activities that will interest you and help you balance the demands of your academic life and gain some practical experience at the same time, especially if you assume a leadership position or participate in various projects throughout the year.

- **How you can benefit from attending the organization's conventions and conferences.** Your membership may enable you to register for such events at a reduced rate. This will do a lot for your morale, and you will often find the presentations and exhibits to be interesting and informative, and that they relate well to your graduate work and your chosen career.

Tip #22: Designing Your Curriculum Vitae (CV) or Résumé the Right Way

You will make use of this document throughout your career, and you will often need to breathe new life into it by including new experiences and accomplishments, such as earning your MBA, and deleting any items that are no longer relevant. You should review your résumé whenever you submit it for any purpose, whether you are looking for a job or applying for membership in an organization, to ensure that it will serve the purpose.

Here are some tips for compiling a résumé that will do exactly what you want it to:

- Learn how to compile a chronological résumé. This type of document should be arranged in reverse chronological order, meaning that if you are job hunting, for example, you will begin by listing your current or most recent position. Never lose sight of the fact that honesty, neatness, and readability count. With this in mind, when discussing your participation in some activity or project, be sure that your description is not embellished or confusing to the reader in any way.

- Your résumé should never be lengthy, must always be well organized, and should be accompanied by a cover letter to complement the general information it contains. As a guide in completing your résumé, you may want to visit **http://www.cvtips.com/CV_example.html** and use one of the templates available there.

Why Cover Letters Matter When You Are Job Hunting

Every cover letter you write is intended to highlight your qualifications for a *particular position* that a potential employer has open, indicating clearly why that company should hire you to fill the job. It is a valuable marketing tool, and should be convincing, relatively brief, and given the attention it deserves. Your cover letter should also show your creativity and leave no doubt in the reader's mind that you feel the job is meant for you. Unless you are writing to a post office box listed in the classified section of a newspaper or professional journal and the name of the related company is unknown, you can indicate that you are familiar with the company doing the hiring and show how your academic training and work experience have prepared you to fill the position in question.

Tip #23: How You Can Catch the Attention of Business Recruiters Online

You may feel that contacting recruiters online may be worth the effort, and you have nothing to lose by making the attempt, but you also need to remember that many other well-qualified people are doing the same thing. Once you realize this, you will see that the trick is to make your résumé stand out from the rest. Here are some ways you can accomplish this:

- **Make an effort to see things from their perspective.** Since recruiters have to go through hundreds of résumés on a daily basis, they tend to separate them by keywords, which can vary, and then correlate them with the slots they have to fill or file them for future reference. In addition, the terms mentioned more than once in a job description posted on the Internet by a recruiting firm are often of special importance here. and you will want to react to them.

- **You have about 30 seconds to capture a recruiter's attention.** Experts in the field of recruitment tell us that this is the standard, and the person who receives your résumé will continue to read it for a maximum of three minutes if it seems interesting. With this in mind, while you want to emphasize your skills and experience and make good use of keywords, you should also respond to the specifics found in the related job description.

- **Find out what others have to say about your résumé before you submit it.** Draw up a list of about five impartial readers, remove your name so that they can be objective, and ask them to critique it. Tell them you want know what caught their attention, what seemed boring to them, and what gave them a negative reaction. Then you can make the necessary changes and proceed to post your résumé online.

- **Use strategy in timing your online résumé postings.** There are seasonal lulls during the end-of-the-year holidays and the months of July and August, when hiring managers and recruiters are not quite so rushed, and your résumé will be given more attention.

- **Think about creating an e-portfolio to use in your job search.** You may want to publish a multifaceted collection of your work online to highlight your accomplishments, goals, philosophy, and experience, which will enable you to become part of a vast social network of like-minded people. In creating it, you will depict who you are by discussing your past life, where you are today, and what you plan to accomplish in the future. Here is how you can go about doing this:

1. Even if you are not a technical wizard and want to compile your portfolio, you can make use of the tools available today, including e-portfolio at **www.eportfolio.org**, Digication at **www.digication.com**, Blogger at **www.blogger.com**, and PBwiki at **www.pbwiki.com**.

2. You want your portfolio to be as polished, professional, and impressive as your résumé. Be sure to use a readable font when you put it together. Include some brief introductions or snippets that easily lead the reader to the complete descriptions and examples you provide, which are the heart of your portfolio. Remember to use keywords throughout the text to increase the number of "hits" you receive, and include links (2 to 5 megabytes) to related topics for added interest. Finally, mention the Web address of this file on your résumé or in your cover letter whenever you send out material related to your job search.

Tip #24: Learn Where You Should Post Your Résumé Online

When you are in the market for a job, especially if you are still employed but want to make a change, you can try posting your résumé at **CareerBuilder.com** or a similar job-search Web site in order to reach a number of potential employers, but there are also some precautions you should take. Here are a few basic points to remember if you decide to do this:

- Try using trusted industry association sites, and make sure you agree with the applicable privacy policy, which you should find posted at the site, making sure that the operator will not share or sell your personal information without your consent.

- Expect to be offered various privacy options as a sign the site is legitimate. For instance, a *Standard* listing may permit employers to search for your résumé through its database, an *Anonymous* listing may allow you to remove all or part of your contact information from your résumé, and a *Privacy* listing will make your résumé unsearchable while permitting you to apply for jobs at the site.

- There are some risks attached to taking this step, since the database is public, and someone from your current company may discover it online. Since this is the case, the site you choose should have certain tools available that will permit you to determine who will see your résumé.

- If you decide to take the risk, do not reveal your private information — including your bank account, driver's license, and credit card numbers — to a potential employer before a formal interview is scheduled, even when you are pressured to do so. If you run into this problem, get in touch with the Better Business Bureau to check out the status of the organization, and find out if any complaints have been lodged against them because of their practices.

Tip #25: How to Make the Most of a Job Interview

When you have a job interview lined up, do not make the

mistake of waiting until the night before to prepare for the big event. As is the case with taking a major test like the GMAT, the more organized you are at the time, the less stressed you will be. Here are some steps you should take to ensure that your interview will go well:

- **Take the time to research your potential employer.** You can do this by visiting the company's Web site for an overview, including the company's mission statement and other key factors that are highlighted. If time permits, speak to any contacts you may have who have inside knowledge and can supply the essential information you need. This will help you to show that you are a knowledgeable job candidate with a definite contribution to make if you are hired.

- **Be sure that you are familiar with what the job entails.** A job title only tells you so much, and the fact that you are being called in does not necessarily mean that you are "perfect" for the position. Be prepared to ask any questions you have during the interview, because you will want to know exactly what you are getting into and what will be expected of you if you accept the job.

- **Some job interviews are conducted over the phone.** They are used as a prescreening device to determine if job applicants are truly interested in a position, can meet its requirements, and should be called in for a formal interview. They also come unexpectedly, and when they do, try to give the interviewer your complete attention and pretend you are meeting face to face.

- **Show your enthusiasm for the job.** During your interview, let your responses to your interviewer's questions, and the questions you ask yourself, show that you are genuinely interested in the position they are filling and in the organization as a whole. When your meeting draws to a close, summarize your feelings about the job and the organization, thank the interviewer for seeing you, and determine what the next step will be.

- **Prepare a career presentation to be used at your interview.** When you prepare for your job interview, and if you are not looking for an entry-level management position, consider assembling a career presentation, a kind of visual aid you can use when you meet with your prospective employer. To achieve its desired purpose, make sure that it is professional and well focused, and include the following elements:

1. **Highlight your accomplishments.** This is the time for you to be creative and document the success you have realized in the past. You can include special awards, performance reviews, or anything similar indicating that you are more than capable of doing the job and doing it well.

2. **Include some photos related to your accomplishments and some of the projects you have worked on.** You can use them as a starting point in your discussion with the interviewer. Make sure that these pictures, including any that are digital, are of good quality.

3. **Stress various projects you have worked on in your**

presentation. Along with the photos, include any pertinent documentation and details related to those projects to add credibility to your message. This will indicate that you are detail-oriented and thorough, which will impress your interviewer.

4. **Make sure that your presentation will go smoothly.** Since your interviewer's time will be limited, organize your material into a comprehensive set of file folders that you can access easily (within ten seconds per item), thus avoiding any awkward, stressful moments when the two of you meet.

Obviously, preparing your career presentation will take time and effort, and you will want to practice with a friend or family member beforehand, but when you consider that it can make the difference between being hired or not, it also falls into the category of a "no brainer."

Tip #26: What You Need to Know About Background Checks

Many employers use them because some job candidates embellish the information contained in their résumé, particularly in regard to their educational background. These companies want to determine if any significant problems can be found in an applicant's past, whether they are related to that person's employment or personal background. Since this is the situation many job hunters have to deal with in the marketplace today, here are some things that may help:

- While large companies conduct thousands of background checks on a daily basis, and this is an additional expense for them, federal law states that this can only be done with an applicant's written authorization. Also, if that applicant is rejected because of something negative contained in that report, he or she must be given an explanation.

- In regard to criminal history, such searches can be done on a national, state, or county basis for information that is of public record. Civil history also can be traced on a similar basis, indicating whether the applicant was a defendant or plaintiff in the case being reported. If you have ever been the victim of identity theft, this part of your background check may contain false information, and you will want to clarify the matter at once. If you feel this may be an issue for you, consider visiting **www.mybackgroundcheck. com** and conducting one on yourself for a nominal fee. Then, if you find any errors in the report, you will be able to correct them using the "Consumer Resources" link.

- A job candidate's credit report is often part of the background check because employers want to hire people who are financially stable, but bankruptcies older than seven years will not be included in that report, and that individual's social security report will indicate where he or she has lived for the past seven years as well. About 15 to 20 percent of such reports also include a drug test, and some organizations have the policy of frequently screening their managers for drugs.

Tip #27: How to Avoid Taking a Job with the Wrong Company

Some companies have serious internal problems of one kind or another, and you certainly would not accept a job offer from them if you were aware of the situation. At the same time, you may feel that time is working against you in your job search if you are unemployed and want to find a new job quickly. Yet, under any circumstances, you will not want to take a job in desperation, and you will need some reassurance that agreeing to take the position will have a positive outcome. Here are some pointers you can use as a guide in accomplishing that:

- **Be specific in deciding what kind of job you want.** As you hunt for a job, consider such factors as the need to relocate, the size of the staff you will manage, the length of your commute, the need to travel on business, the possibility for advancement, and how you feel about each one. Then you can be guided by your basic intuition as you go about your search.

- **Ask the right questions during your interview.** When it comes to work-related issues that concern you, ask specific, detailed questions that cannot be answered with a simple "yes" or "no." You may also want to go beyond the parameters of the formal job description related to the position in order to determine exactly what the job entails and what will be expected of you on a daily basis if you accept it.

- **Speak to others who already work for the organization if you can.** If you are used to professional networking, you may have one or more contacts who will be in a position to give you the information you need, and if one of them told you about the job opening in the first place, that would be a good sign. If you are unfamiliar with the area or are changing careers, your interviewer should be willing to have you speak to some of the people who will be your colleagues; if that is not the case, this may be a sign that all is not well there.

Tip #28: What You Should Know About Corporate Culture

Corporate culture, which may be summarized in a company's mission statement, underlies the group's values and general outlook, which all employees are expected to adopt. In addition, it strongly affects the decision-making process that is in place, although this is not always realized until changes are about to take place. Here are a few tips related to corporate culture:

1. **What corporate culture does.** It provides the employees with a sense of well-being, and it is intended to strengthen the individual's identification with and commitment to the employer through the leadership of its managers. It also serves two essential purposes:

   - **It unites the group internally.** Ideally, corporate culture creates a collective sense of identity and enables employees to communicate more easily with one another.

   - **It enables the group as a whole to adjust to external**

forces. The formation of a corporate culture makes it easier to cope with competitors, meet the needs of their customers and the demands of the marketplace, and carry out long-term goals.

2. **Corporate cultures may be grouped into four major categories.** As you go about your job search, you will want to determine which category has the greatest appeal for you and which category is represented by a potential employer. They are as follows:

- **Entrepreneurial.** These companies are proactive, flexible, and concerned with meeting their customers' needs.

- **Mission.** These organizations concentrate on carrying out their original purpose, serve a specific customer base, and do not favor rapid change.

- **Clan.** These groups focus on the rapid changes taking place in today's world and the need of their employees to adapt to those changes successfully.

- **Bureaucratic.** These corporations value conformity, consistency, and collaboration in their internal operations and expect to reach their goals through the implementation of the policies and procedures they establish.

Tip #29: What You Can Do as a Manager to Increase Your Earning Potential

If you want to succeed as a manager, move up the ladder in your organization, and increase your earning power, an employee's benefit package often equals about 42 percent of his or her annual salary. Thus, to increase your earning potential, keep the following suggestions in mind:

1. **Be sure that you hear what your boss is saying to you.** Enthusiasm for what you are doing and impressive productivity are fine, but you also want to determine what your company's priorities are, along with those of your boss. "Chain of command" is a time-honored term in many fields, and once you are in a management position, those who are in upper-level management will expect the same cooperation from you that you expect from the people you supervise. If you ever feel unsure about a specific action or its timing, do not hesitate to ask your boss for clarification and use those communication skills you developed while earning your MBA.

2. **Know exactly what your medical benefits are.** Regardless of the medical coverage you have through your employer, consult the benefits summary for information on plan options, applicable premiums, and covered services. If you are new on the job, you will want to know if you can cover your dependents, when coverage will begin, and if preexisting conditions apply. Since the average insurance premium cost outpaces employees' earnings and the inflation rate, many insurers offer less costly plan options accompanied by reduced coverage, and you will want to be aware of this. Note also that high-deductible plans come with a lower premium and coverage for "catastrophic events," but this type of medical insurance does not suit everyone's needs.

3. **Keep your performance goals in mind, and you will be happy with your annual bonus.** The performance bonus is an opportunity offered by a majority of companies to their top executives and managers on every level, and the size of your annual bonus will be based on the quality of your job performance throughout the year. With this in mind, discuss your goals in detail at the time of your annual review so that the size of your bonus will not be determined on an arbitrary basis and you will feel that you are being treated fairly.

4. **Get sound financial advice from an expert.** While you may be able to handle budget matters in your department quite skillfully, you may not have the time or the inclination to give your personal finances all the attention they deserve. If this is your situation, you may be in need of financial counseling so that you will know what to do with your stock options (if applicable), retirement plan, and other financial benefits.

5. **Find out if any special commissions or awards are available to you.** Many companies offer one or both of these "perks," and they also pay a one-time bonus to someone on the staff who refers candidates for vacant positions that are hard to fill or who is able to bring in new business.

6. **Take advantage of your company's 401(k) plan.** Determine if your employer will match your contribution to this retirement savings account, up to a certain level If this is so, you should keep long-term growth in mind, since it should be the deciding factor. For example, your company may contribute half of the amount you contribute until that

amount equals 6 percent of your salary or $1,500 annually for an individual earning $50,00 per year.

7. **Make use of your tax-free income through your employer.** Your human resources department will inform you if they offer flexible-spending accounts that can be used to cover the expense of healthcare, commuting, and child care with pretax dollars. You will have less take-home pay if you participate in this program, but you will benefit on April 15, because the amount of your federal taxable income will be lowered by the amount that has been deducted from your salary.

8. **Know where to find reliable salary information to prepare for interviews and salary negotiation.** Once you have your MBA, and throughout your career, you will want to know where to find reliable salary information for your own purposes and to use when answering your employees' questions. Here are some reliable sources that should prove to be helpful in doing this:

   - To research salary information for a particular region in the United States, visit the Career Builders calculator at **http://www.cbsalary.com.**Such Web sites often base their data on location, academic background, and years of work experience.

   - The government's Bureau of Labor Statistics (BLS) at **http://www.bls.gov compiles data on national trends**, including current unemployment rates and individual occupations. In addition, its Occupational Outlook Handbook at **www.bls.gov/oco/home.htm** includes job descriptions, their related qualifications and working conditions, average wages, and the current employment outlook.

- Consult various industry publications and Web sites for a broad picture of what those seeking a management position in your area can expect at the present time. If you are willing to relocate to accept a new job, you will want to consult Monster.com's cost-of-living calculator at **http://salary.monster.com/CostOfLivingWizard/ layoutscripts/coll_start.asp**. This financial tool will enable you to input a particular metropolitan area, provide an overview of all living expenses, and show you if moving there would result in an actual increase or decrease in your yearly income.

Tip #30: What You Can Do When Faced with a Company Merger

Mergers and acquisitions have become fairly commonplace in many industries today, and there is no indication that the trend will die out any time soon. Since this is the situation, you will need to be prepared for this possibility throughout your career. If your organization is affected at some point, you would be foolish to assume that your job is not in jeopardy. Here are some tips for handling such a situation and coming out ahead:

- **Be aware of what happens when companies merge.** Taking this step is often a cost-saving measure on the part of the administration, and you may discover that your job is being eliminated. If this happens, make it clear to top management that you want to stay within the organization, even if that means taking on new responsibilities and a new job title. This will show that you are not in denial, that you are flexible and thinking positively, and that you are willing to adjust to the change. You will also need to make sure that you are familiar with the latest trends in your field in order to be convincing, and you may want to do some research online before you speak with them.

- **Your résumé will serve a new purpose at that point.** You are likely in the habit of updating it periodically as a precaution, but during the merger, you will want to ensure top management from the "new" company that you are someone they need. To do this effectively, you will need to research that organization online, just as if you were preparing for a job interview, learn all you can about them, and determine where you might fit in under the new regime. If you also deal with your company's human resources department at that time, be certain that the information you are given is complete and accurate, and accept the fact that you may need to relocate because of the merger.

Tip #31: How to Tell When You Should Start Looking for Another Job

The tell-tale signs indicating that a company is planning to downsize are often evident long before any official announcements are made. If they become obvious in your organization, you will want to start looking for a new job long before your current one comes to an end. If you like your present job, you will face this realization with mixed emotions because you will also be trying to show your boss that you are too valuable for the company to lose.

These are some steps you should take if you feel your job is in jeopardy:

1. **Try to determine if you might be laid off in the foreseeable future.** Here are some indications that you should plan to move on, make sure that your résumé is up to date, and start job hunting without feeling guilty:

   - Your employer initiates a hiring freeze, either in your department or throughout the organization.

   - New procedures are established related to vacation time, expense accounts, or other benefits often referred to as "perks." This is often done in an effort to cut expenses.

   - Your company's current earnings are flat or declining, and its stock has landed on the "strong sell" list.

   - A merger of some sort is in effect or scheduled to take place. This is often done to improve the bottom line and create a "reduction in force."

   - The job market is sluggish in your area, or the industry as a whole is declining.

2. **Instead of acting like a victim, be proactive if your employer downsizes.** This is the time to make use of your networking skills and update your résumé. If you wait until the axe falls, you may find that much of the information you have in your list of contacts is out of date and that

you allow your negative feelings at the time to sabotage that update. It will be much easier and far less awkward to bring home pertinent information from work while you are still on the job than trying to request it after you leave and start looking for a new job.

3. **Try to stay calm if you are told you will be out of a job.** Even if you are escorted from the building, which is often standard procedure now, show as little emotion as possible when dealing with your boss or your coworkers. Doing this will enable you to negotiate your severance package carefully and help you avoid signing anything in haste that you might later regret. If your company is large or going through a series of layoffs, a clearly established severance policy may be in place and negotiation will not be an option for you.

4. **You will also be eligible for unemployment compensation.** As a rule, you will be able to start collecting unemployment when your monthly severance payments come to an end, and you should not hesitate to exercise that option. In addition, since certain expenses related to your job search will be tax-deductible, you should keep track of them in order to comply with Internal Revenue Service (IRS) regulations.

Tip #32: How You Can Tell if You Are Suffering from Job Burnout

This condition — which our ancestors felt was the result of "burning the candle at both ends" — develops gradually, and like many other illnesses, it should be caught in the early stages when it is easier to cure. Job burnout can result in a variety of physical illnesses and cause a tremendous amount of emotional distress, and while many of its victims may be in denial, it is relatively common in our fast-paced society.

As you cope with the duties of work, family, and perhaps graduate courses simultaneously, these are the signs of job burnout you should look for:

- While you may not necessarily erupt in outbursts of anger, you discover that you are becoming increasingly irritable and impatient with others at home and on the job.

- It is difficult to get yourself to work on time, and you find yourself resisting the impulse to leave at least a few minutes early at the end of the day. In addition, you have lost your enthusiasm for the job, never look for new challenges, and any type of networking has lost its appeal.

- You also do not feel well physically. This may include difficulty sleeping, headaches, and feeling exhausted, all of which are signs that you are suffering from job stress. If this is happening to you, see what adjustments you can make to ease the situation, including delegating some work to your staff or getting permission to extend the deadline of a project you are working on, if possible. As you study the situation in detail, you may come to the conclusion that it is time for you to look for another job.

Tip #33: What You Should Do When You Decide to Leave One Job for Another

There is an element of truth in the old saying that you should never "burn your bridges behind you," and if you decide to change jobs, you will need to notify your employer that you are taking this step at a time when you may be experiencing mixed emotions and not thinking too clearly. Here are some suggestions to follow when you find yourself in that situation:

- Act professionally and courteously when leaving an employer, and inform your supervisor of your decision before telling your colleagues and staff. At a minimum, this should be done two weeks before your departure.

- Avoid any sign of boasting, thank people for their support and interest, and exchange contact information in order to network with them in the future.

- Compose a formal letter of resignation that is brief, courteous, and clearly states that you intend to leave. Do this at least two weeks in advance so that your employer can begin looking for your replacement. In addition, make it clear to your future employer that you want to do this in order to avoid confusion and as a sign of your professionalism.

- Make sure that things are in good order, leave a good lasting impression, avoid gossiping with malcontents, and indicate clearly what remains to be done after you are gone. If time permits, offer to train your replacement before you go.

- At your exit interview, take the time to negotiate your severance package carefully, but avoid bringing up problems that you should have mentioned earlier and decided not to for one reason or another.

Tip #34: What to Do When You Have to Relocate to Accept a New Job

Packing and moving into a new home is always stressful, and you may find that you are dealing with this situation at a time when you are also adjusting to a new job — and all that goes with it if you accept a job offer that involves relocating. Here are some things you will want to consider before you take that step:

- **Determine if relocating will be good for your family.** If you are moving far from your current home, take the time to become familiar with the new location and see what it has to offer in the way of job opportunities for your spouse, if that applies. When you visit the area, focus on the housing situation, the school system, and the cost of living there, which consists of many factors, including local, state, and property taxes.

- **Find out if you will be reimbursed for your moving expenses.** If, after arming yourself with this information, you feel ready to accept the job offer and relocate, you will want to know which of your moving expenses will be taken care of by your new employer, including those involved in visiting the area beforehand to check out the available housing and determine where you are going to live. Ideally, such policies will be outlined for you in written form and you will be able to verify them in a way that is satisfactory. In addition, you will want to know exactly when you will be reimbursed so that you can keep your finances in order.

If you travel by car to get to your destination, your employer may have established rules about the number of miles you must travel in a single day and the number of days allowed for making the trip. Under all circumstances, remember to keep the receipts related to all your travel expenses, both large and small, for your relocation because some of them will be tax-deductible. You can find additional information regarding your relocation expenses by visiting by visiting the IRS Web site at **http://www.irs.gov/publications/p521/ar01. html**.

Tip #35: What You Should Expect When You Start a New Job

If you are hired or promoted to a new management position, you may find that the opening was newly created, which will present its own opportunities and concerns. Yet, it is more likely that you will be taking the place of a highly regarded individual who has moved on or retired and who is sorely missed by at least some of your employees. Here are some suggestions for helping your staff and others to adjust to the change and establishing your position at the same time:

- If you are frustrated because of something your predecessor did or did not do and feel the temptation to voice your criticism, try to keep your emotions in check. You will be an unknown quantity at that point, and your unguarded comments about people who are not there to defend themselves will only cause the listener to feel antagonistic toward you.

- Place the changes you want to make in the order of their priority, and be sure to introduce them slowly. This will give people time to adjust to everything that is happening, which will be sorely needed, and they will feel reassured in knowing that you are not acting hastily.

- Consult with your staff to build a new coalition. Have them explain why certain procedures were established by your predecessor, see if they feel that any of them need to set aside or updated, and show that you are open to any suggestions they may have. At the same time, you should also make it clear that "business as usual" will not be your motto.

Conclusion

Even in the best of circumstances, your career in management will not proceed at an even pace. With this in mind, here are a few things for you to consider:

- The many different fields where your management skills can be applied.

- The importance of networking, joining professional organizations, and keeping your résumé updated.

- The possibility of creating an e-portfolio as a job-hunting tool.

- Knowing where corporate culture fits in and what to do in a company merger.

- Deciding when you need to look for another job and recognizing the symptoms of burnout.

- How to handle relocating for a new job.

Chapter 3
What Attending Graduate School Will Be Like

While you may be interested in earning an MBA, you will also want to have a clear picture of what you will be getting into when you apply to graduate school. What follows should help provide it.

Tip #36: What You Should Expect from a Business School Program

You may be surprised to learn that most MBA programs differ from other graduate school divisions, because they often do not require applicants to have completed an undergraduate program in the field of study they pursue when working toward an advanced degree. This also explains why you will not be tested in any particular area of specialization when taking the GMAT.

You will find your fellow students and the faculty will come from a wide range of educational and work-related experiences. In the classroom, you will have contact with tenured faculty; adjunct faculty, who deal daily with today's workplace; and guest lecturers. Also, your participation in student activities, community-based programs, and international tours may prove to be an essential part of your graduate school experience. Here are some of the things you can expect:

1. **What your fellow students in business school will be like.** The people in your graduate program may have been trained in business, engineering, or the social sciences; or they may have a liberal arts degree. They will also be somewhat competitive. Many of them will have at least a few years of valuable work experience, and you should be prepared to cooperate with them in group projects as an essential part of this learning experience. Be aware that your post-graduate options will be based on your pre-MBA practical experience, and postpone enrolling if you realize you are not ready to pursue an advanced degree.

2. **What your attitude toward competition in class should be.** The spirit of competitiveness you find in graduate school, which is sometimes exaggerated, is a function of that institution's culture, and business school cultures can vary significantly in this regard. The topic of competitiveness is a complex one that is sometimes overemphasized in regard to any type of advanced study and the business world. In addition, something that is known as "healthy competition" often results when students try hard to do their best and challenge each other; most potential MBAs tend to compete in that way. Cultivating this spirit, of course, will prove to be an asset on the job as well.

3. **What to do if you have a non-business undergraduate degree and want to get an MBA.** If you are in this situation, you can still bring your worthwhile viewpoints and experiences to your graduate classes and be acceptable to future employers. Once you have completed your MBA

program, your prior background will not be considered extremely important by most employers, because the core curriculum courses in your graduate program, your elective courses, and any work experience you may gain while earning your MBA will supply the business training you need and help you to sharpen your business skills.

4. **Why the composition of graduate school faculties may vary.** The typical business school works to achieve a delicate balance between research, which fosters up-to-date course content, and teaching methodology, which strengthens its ties to industry, and it aims to attract its faculty on that basis. Student-to-teacher ratio is another significant factor you should consider when deciding where to earn your MBA, since the core curriculum classes can be quite large at times.

5. **The role research will play in your graduate program.** Business schools often place a lot of emphasis on research, feeling that it helps improve their course content, among other things, and this can be to your advantage as a student who has an opportunity to participate in it. Conversely, if such a policy prevails at a given institution, limited interaction with students on the part of the faculty may be an unfortunate side effect of this trend.

When this is not the case and those on the faculty are not living with the mantra of "publish or perish," you may find an environment that is rich in opportunities for learning as you complete your graduate program. In an ideal situation, where research and teaching complement each other, you may become involved in the research projects of one or more of your professors, experience satisfying interaction in class, and share in the good reputation that your business school enjoys.

6. **Making good use of the school's library as you study.** To complete your research projects and class assignments more easily, become familiar with the many resources available there, and make good use of them. Such facilities often provide students with free access to large databases, which will enable you to produce impressive work for your classes that is of professional quality.

7. **Knowing what the typical MBA graduate is like today.** A study done by the U.S. Department of Education reveals that students in American MBA schools are more diverse than those enrolled in any other master's program in the country. One common characteristic they share is that they all believe gaining an MBA will help them to realize their personal goals, especially in regard to their career.

Along with representatives from other fields, many of these students have experience in the nonprofit sector, marketing, engineering, consulting, copywriting, technology, auditing, and research, and, of course, they also possess an aptitude for management. As a rule, the salary they earn after graduating is based on their work experience, their business school transcript, and the country's economic climate at the time.

8. **Estimating what your future income will be if you get an MBA.** You can begin by researching the published college-placement salary statistics of recent graduates to determine how successful business school alumni are in advancing their careers and how the business world values the education received from a particular institution. These statistics are listed by average years of experience, industry, function, and geographical area, indicating that the related cost-of-living expenses will vary accordingly. In

addition, you will want to know the percentage of MBA graduates from that school who received job offers, how the information was gathered, and when those statistics were compiled to determine their validity.

Tip #37: Part-time Graduate Study Programs for Those Who Work Full-time

If you choose this option, you will find that many programs conduct classes in the evening or on Saturday, and you will need to adjust your social and family life. You will also want to continue to be productive at work while taking on a reasonable course load. On the plus side, you can check with your employer's human resources department to see if the company has a tuition reimbursement program and if you have been on the staff long enough to qualify for it. Note that nearly every program of this type comes with a monetary "cap" of some sort, including the allotment of a certain dollar amount per semester or credit hour.

You should also weigh the following positive and negative factors before making your decision about combining full-time employment with graduate study:

- **The advantages of studying on a part-time basis.** The courses that are part of such programs are designed for professionals who work full time and want to enhance their careers by earning an advanced degree. In a program like this, you can increase your expertise and continue your current employment at the same time, and you will gradually learn to solve the "real-world" problems you encounter on the job by applying what you are learning in your business school classes.

- **The negative aspects of studying on a part-time basis.** Scholarship money may not be available as part of such a program, and you may find that the school's placement office is closed when you are on campus to attend class. The latter situation may present quite a problem if you are planning on looking for a new employer once you have your advanced degree, but doing some networking may compensate here.

Tip #38: Your Military Experience Can Count When You Apply to Business School

If you have a military background, you will find that a number of schools are receptive to having you in their MBA program and helping you advance your career. Often, they will waive the application fee for those who have been on active duty in the military during the previous three years, if state and institutional regulations permit doing so, and they also make a special effort to provide financial aid for qualified individuals who have left the military within the previous two years. In addition, they will grant a one-year deferment to students already admitted into the program whose plans are delayed by military issues, such as redeployment overseas.

You also will have some important factors working in your favor because of your military background:

- **You will have an advantage when you enroll in business school.** Many of these institutions want to inform you about their MBA programs and help you advance your career, make the best possible use of your military experience, and explain the benefits that are available to you if you enroll. For detailed descriptions of pertinent individual schools and programs throughout the country in alphabetical order, visit **www.mba.com**.

- **You can look into Operation MBA, which focuses on those who have military experience.** Through its program known as Operation MBA, the Graduate Management Admission Council (GMAC®) is speaking to military personnel — both active-duty and reserve — and civilians who are in military-support positions about the fact that military experience and a graduate degree in business is a valued combination. They also stress that people with military experience can bring a unique perspective to any MBA program because of their background.

If you have military experience and would like more information about this particular program, you can reach GMAC's Customer Service Department online at **http://www.gmac.com/gmac/Service/ContactUs.htm? type=operationmba**. You can also call +1-703-245-4222, if you are stationed outside the country, or 1-866-505-6559, which is toll-free within the United States and Canada.

- **You may also have an advantage when looking for a job as a civilian.** A number of companies are military-friendly because they feel that people with a military background have developed the "team player" and leadership skills they are looking for in their managers, along with the ability to perform under pressure, technological expertise, and personal integrity.

As you apply for a job at a particular company, you will find that making a convincing comparison between the skills that were required during your years in the military and those needed to fill the position they have open is quite a challenge. To help you in accomplishing this, try visiting O*NET OnLine at **http://online.onetcenter.org**. This is a specialized tool that you can use to align Dictionary of Occupational Titles (DOT) or Maritime Operations Center (MOC) codes with related non-military positions by job title and job description. Also, since most companies in the private sector are not familiar with the jargon used by military personnel, you will have to indicate clearly on your résumé and in your interviews that your skills are fresh and transferable.

- **Make use of the employment information intended for veterans that you can find online.** As you research the job opportunities available to people with military experience, go to OperationHeroforHire.com at **http://www.jobpath.com/ csh/search.aspx?csh=CSH_OHFH&cbRecursion Cnt=2&cbsid=1552b9afdc56422da3695eb545a11 79c-255645727-JA-5**, the President's National Hire Veterans Committee at **http://www.hirevetsfirst. gov/committee.asp**,Veterans Employment and Training at **http://www.dol.gov/vets**, and other related Web sites.

Tip #39: Opportunities for Studying Abroad as You Earn Your MBA in the United States

As diversity becomes increasingly important in the business world, many graduate students include studying abroad as part (or all) of their program to gain greater access to the positions they are preparing to fill. In line with this are a number of summer graduate-study programs that are geared toward helping future MBAs prepare to take their place in today's global economy and function effectively wherever they may be.

You can participate in a month-long study session in the summer that will familiarize you with the region *formally* during the week, with intense tutorials that will help you feel more comfortable when you take the GMAT, and *informally* on weekends by providing opportunities for you to travel. This experience (along with even shorter foreign courses that are interspersed throughout the MBA program schedule) includes courses in current marketing strategies, sound business practices, free trade, and international business ethics.

Tip #40: Opportunities for Earning Your MBA Outside of the United States

Since the global economy has now become a reality, many American students are considering attending an international business school to earn their MBA degree because they want to focus on global business theory and experience living in a multicultural population abroad. Overseas, the Institut Européen d'Administration des Affaires (INSEAD) in France and the International Institute for Management Development (IMD) in Switzerland have many applicants from the United States, along with the well-known London Business School (LBS) and the Rotterdam School of Management (RSM).

As you set about deciding where to pursue your MBA, note that studying abroad will hold a special attraction for you if you have one or more of these goals as part of your long-range career plan:

- **You want to experience cultural diversity on a firsthand basis.** You will find this in the student body if you study overseas, and your business school training should help you develop your international management skills and prepare to be an international executive. RSM, for example, attracts students from Asia and the Middle East, Central and South America, and Mexico, and only about 4 percent of its students are from the Netherlands.

- **You want to continue your career abroad once you have your MBA.** Today, many well-known American businesses do their share of recruiting at international business schools, and being there as a student could be to your advantage if you want to work outside the United States once you have your degree.

- **You want to become more proficient in a foreign language and make use of bilingual job opportunities.** The Haute Ecole de Commerce in France and the Escuela Superior de Administración y Dirección de Empresas (ESADE) in Spain run bilingual programs, and even if the international program you choose is not bilingual, you will acquire a general knowledge of the local language of the country where your business school is based because of the exposure this experience will provide for you.

Tip #41: Getting an MBA if You Are Interested in Project Management as a Career

Project managers are always in demand, whether they work full-time for a particular organization or decide to become consultants. They are often considered crucial to the success of a company, and their usual task is to plan, carry out, and evaluate significant projects that their group undertakes on behalf of their employer or client.

Being a bit like a juggler keeping several balls in the air simultaneously, a good project manager will oversee the key factors of any scheduled project, including the available resources, the amount of money budgeted for the project, the amount of time allotted to complete the project, and, most important of all, the project's scope. If this is the career path you want to prepare for, your MBA training will guide you in doing the following:

- **Managing the scope of the project you are assigned.** A project's main ingredients are the expected results and the means that will be used to achieve those goals. Any significant alteration in the scope of the project, once it has been undertaken, will often require an automatic adjustment to the amount of time, money, and resources needed to complete it successfully. If these adjustments are not possible, or if they are vetoed in some way, the wise project manager will be adamant about leaving the original scope of the project intact. This is the key to managing the project resources — the people, labor subcontractors (if any), equipment, and material needed to complete the job effectively and as scheduled.

- **Managing the people who work on the project.** This task includes having the personnel with the necessary skills to do the job and providing them with the tools they need when they need them to avoid any production delays. The staff also needs to know what is expected of them, how long they have to do the job, and why they should be enthused about the project as part of the team. Ordinarily, a project manager directs the supervisor in each group of employees taking part in the project and the supervisor of any subcontract workers involved in it as well.

- **Managing the equipment used in completing the project.** This can vary, depending on the nature of the project, but in every case, you will need to have the necessary equipment, operating properly, where it is needed, and when it is needed.

- **Making sure that you complete the project on time.** Good managers know that sticking to the project schedule means they are working to ensure they stay within the project budget, because poor time management is the most likely cause of overspending on a project. Software is now available to assist them in managing their project timeline and overlapping tasks, if that becomes necessary.

- **Learning to compile a project schedule to ensure a successful outcome.** To complete this essential task, a project manager must determine what subtasks the project requires, the order in which they should be done, and the amount of time and the resources that will be needed to complete each step of the project as planned.

When a project schedule is complete, you will find that some tasks listed are a bit flexible in regard to their start and completion date, a factor often referred to as "float." A line can be drawn through tasks that lack this flexibility, and that line is known as the "critical path" of a project. This means the project manager will have to focus on this critical path in order for the project to succeed while monitoring the other tasks listed on the project schedule.

As the project takes shape, certain tasks may be removed from the "critical path" or added to it as unforeseen circumstances come up, including a delay in the shipment of materials or the unanticipated hiring of additional workers.

- **Staying within the project's budget and watching the bottom line.** Every task that is part of the project will involve some expense, and when the actual cost of a budget item is unknown, a "design allowance" is included in the budget in case it varies widely from the original estimated cost. A contingency amount is also provided as an emergency measure to allow for unpredictable events, such as difficulties with vendors or bad weather. The project manager's goal here is to keep the actual cost of the project at or below the original cost estimate and boost the profit the company realizes from it simultaneously.

Tip #42: What You Should Know If You Are an Upper-level Manager Who Is Interested in an Executive MBA (EMBA) Program

This type of program is intended to bring an executive's career to a new level, and it may also be company-sponsored. Those who participate in such a program are often business veterans with a minimum of five years' experience in their particular specialty or industry who need to sharpen their managerial skills to be promoted or because they have taken on new responsibilities. With this in mind, their practical experience and professional expertise are always an essential part of any graduate program that is geared toward them.

In view of the typical participant's busy work schedule, EMBA classes tend to meet on alternate weekends, and they complete the program in two years rather than one. Also, because of the unique composition of the group, there is extensive faculty interaction with individual students and groups of students, with their career advancement and opportunities for networking clearly in mind.

Here are some points to consider before you enroll in an EMBA program:

1. **How EMBA programs differ from other graduate programs.** Internships and scholarships are often not

available in these programs because students are full-time employees, but EMBA candidates who are interested in obtaining a student loan can research them at the GMAC Web site, **http://www.gmac.com**. As part of this program, all participants take the same core courses at the same time, as opposed to the more common business-school pattern that schedules general management courses in the first year and elective courses the following year.

If you plan to enroll in this specialized executive course of study, you will need to devote 80 to 100 hours per week to work and study, and absences from class will not be tolerated, since sessions are only held four days out of the month. In this case, students who are sponsored by their employer often do not register with the school's job placement office because a potential conflict-of-interest situation could arise.

2. **What you will get out of completing an EMBA program.** The following are only some of the benefits you will realize from earning your graduate degree:

   - In a business environment that is constantly evolving, this program will enable you to stay up to date as you sharpen your skills and gain knowledge that you will be able to apply on the job.

   - As you go through the course of study, your business insight, along with your analytical and decision-making skills, will improve as you prepare to assume a more significant leadership role in your organization or move on to advance your career.

   - Some programs in this category offer two alternative

tracks: a general EMBA or an EMBA with a specialization in marketing, international relations, or e-business, allowing you to tailor your program to suit your needs and preferences.

3. **The curriculum you will follow in graduate school.** The typical EMBA program has an outstanding curriculum that offers several courses in the essential business disciplines, and it is also an integral part of managerial training. Such a program includes courses in organizational behavior, applied managerial decision making, project management processes in organizations, legal and ethical decision making, applied managerial marketing, leadership, applied accounting for decision making, applied finance for decision making, and information technology for business management.

Tip #43: How to Get an MBA If You Are Interested in Completing an Accelerated Program

This one-year program covers the core MBA curriculum subjects in less time than the traditional business school programs do, and elective courses and provision for specialization are often limited. But if you are interested in studying general management, it can be an effective way to earn a promotion and advance your career.

Since the class schedule is more condensed than that of a two-year program, you will find that attendance is mandatory. Those who do well in this situation often have a foundation in management fundamentals through their work experience and undergraduate studies, and they often already hold a managerial position when they begin the program.

Tip #44: Getting an MBA if You Would Like to Start Your Own Business

If you would like to establish a business of your own, you need to be an expert on the product or service you are offering to your customers or clients, but you should also be familiar with the factors involved in running a successful company, including dealing with your employees, vendors, and clients, and succeeding financially.

Here are two essential points for you to consider if you want to become a consultant or start your own business:

1. **What an MBA degree can do for you as an entrepreneur.** Earning an entrepreneurship MBA can be an excellent way to build the foundation you will need in business management and ventures, and with some programs, you may be able to access investment capital after graduation to finance your new business. In addition, the Small Business Association (SBA) reports that 75 percent of new jobs added to our economy each year are due to the efforts of entrepreneurs.

2. **The courses you will need to take in business school.** While you will study general business subjects — including marketing and budgeting — and will fill many roles as your business grows, you also should focus your attention on product development, managing capital, and international business for entrepreneurs. The Tepper School of Business

at Carnegie Mellon University, which is considered one of America's best business schools, offers an MBA program that may be of special interest to you if you want to become an entrepreneur.

Conclusion

To succeed in getting an MBA, you will want to know what to expect in graduate school, which will be different from your undergraduate experience. You will also want to be aware of:

- Part-time graduate programs for people who work full time.

- Where military experience fits in when applying to business school.

- Opportunities to study abroad and earn your MBA in another country.

- The possibility of becoming a project manager with this degree.

- The EMBA program for executives.

- The accelerated MBA program.

- The value of an MBA for an entrepreneur or consultant.

Chapter 4
Discovering More About the Things Managers Have to Do

Certain activities are part of the day-to-day life of many managers, and you will feel more confident if you have some idea of what they entail before you assume a management position or decide to continue your studies. Descriptions of some of the more significant tasks they perform — and how to handle them — follow.

Tip #45: How to Write an Effective Business Plan for Prospective Investors

If you are an entrepreneur or a manager preparing to market a new product or service, there are many reasons why you should know how to write a comprehensive business plan based on thorough research in order to win the backing and support you need. Doing this will help you see if your idea has any merit and will enable you to stay focused as you try to bring it to life. In addition, you will find that such a plan is essential if you want to interest investors, board members or donors, secure a business loan, or apply for a government grant.

- **Part One of Your Business Plan — The Executive Summary**

This is the first section that those who read your plan will see, but you should write it after all the other sections are completed because it is intended to provide them with an overview of what you have in mind. Here are some steps you should follow:

1. **How to complete this section of your plan.** One time-tested method is to write one or two sentences that summarize each section of your business plan and then "seal the deal" with a powerful conclusion to convince the reader that your project is bound to succeed. You will also find it helpful to look at a few sample business plans before you begin to write your own and use them as a guide.

2. **What you should do.** You are just summarizing here. This section should only be one or two pages long, and the tone should be strong and positive in order to capture the reader's interest. Try reading the executive summary aloud to determine what its effect on the reader might be, and ask someone who is objective to read it and comment on its general tone. Above all, you want to make certain that it will get your message across to your intended audience.

- **Part Two of Your Business Plan — Writing About the Industry That Relates to Your Business**

This is made up of two parts:

1. **Provide an overview of that industry at the present time.** In this section, you will want to indicate the industry's size

and scope, its current leaders, and its long-term outlook. You should also discuss the industry's customer base and its estimated sales for the current year as compared to the previous one, and indicate how it is affected by the prevailing economic trends.

2. **Describe your position in that industry.** Tell your audience what products or services you have to offer, why they are unique, and how you will gain entry into the market. Discuss your target market and your chief competitors, and list any patents, franchise rights, copyrights, or trademarks that you already possess or plan to obtain prior to your start-up or launch date.

- **Part Three of Your Business Plan — The Market Analysis**

Even if your business will be a local one, you should describe the people who might be attracted to your product or service, determine how broad your customer base will be, and estimate your anticipated sales volume. Remember to do the following:

1. **Identify the target market for your business.** To begin, you will need to know your target market's age bracket, gender, and location; other variables you should consider include income bracket, family structure, and lifestyle. For the benefit of those who will read your business plan, you should also correctly attribute the sources of your information within this section for greater credibility.

2. **Indicate your projections about that market.** Determine how many people in your target market might turn out to

be repeat customers, whether they will be affected by some demographic shift or loss of employment — such as the closing of a military base — or some larger issue — such as an increase in property taxes or the price of oil. In addition, if you are targeting several groups, you may want to number each one for the sake of clarity as you report on it.

- **Part Four of Your Business Plan — The Competitive Analysis**

On the local level, identifying your competitors will be a relatively simple process, since you can visit their facilities, but you will also be competing with large wholesalers and companies that sell their products online or through their catalogs, and they have to be considered as well. Since this is the case, when you are working on this section, you will want to show the reader that you have "done your homework" by presenting a complete picture. Completing this section is a three-step process:

1. **What you ought to know about your competitors.** Ideally, you should know a competitor's target market, the benefits they offer, and how they attract new clients or customers. In addition, you will want to learn as much as you can about their products or services, their advertising campaigns, and their pricing methods. You can do this by visiting related Web sites and online publications or gathering relevant information from newspapers and magazines.

2. **Analyzing the information you have gathered.** Once you have compiled the data, you will want to decide exactly how you are going to compete with the company in question. Many businesses do this successfully by

identifying a need within a specific target group that is not being met at the time and proceeding to fill that need. (This segment is sometimes referred to as a "market niche.") For example, you may want to offer evening hours if you find that a competitor only does business when many of your potential customers are at work and has no plans to change that schedule.

3. **What you should do next.** As you write your analysis, you will want assure the reader that you are familiar with the competition you will be facing, indicate clearly why you want to compete with those companies, and explain how you intend to build a successful business of your own.

   - **Part Five of Your Business Plan — Your Marketing Strategy**

In this section, explain how you will present your products and services to your potential customers. Indicate the product or service you plan to market, the sales approach you are going to take, the pricing method you will use, and your advertising strategy. All of these steps should be based on the research you have already done in order to be effective. In addition, your goal will be to conduct a series of coordinated promotional activities that will help you reach your targeted market and attract repeat customers. Here is what you will need to do:

1. **Explain what your company has to offer its customers or clients.** Describe the relevant product or service in detail, indicating why it is unique, how it fills a specific need, and how the customer will benefit from it. Some of these benefits may be intangible. For example, a reliable home security system will protect your customers' family and

valuables, but installing it will provide them with a sense of well-being they will not have unless they purchase the item.

2. **Develop your pricing strategy.** As you work on this section, you will determine the price of your product or service while keeping these two factors in mind:

    - You want the price you charge for your product or service to be comparable to that of your competition.

    - You want to realize a reasonable profit, keeping all of your expenses and the demographics of your target market in mind as you calculate what your anticipated return on investment (ROI) will be.

3. **Decide on the distribution methods you will use.** Describe in detail how your product or service will reach your customers and whether you plan to do this via the Internet, through the mail, with sales representatives, or in a retail setting. You should also explain the delivery terms that will apply and the inventory levels you plan to maintain to avoid placing items on "back order."

4. **Decide on the transaction process you will use.** Outline exactly how you will handle order processing, how these orders will be shipped once they are ready, the billing system you plan to use, and the methods of payment you will accept. In addition, indicate what customer service and support you intend to offer, along with your return policy.

5. **Develop a plan for advertising and promoting your**

business. Consider which media you will be using in order to reach your target market, budget accordingly, and indicate your anticipated profit from investing in such advertising. You can also market your product with free samples, discount coupons, and product demonstrations whenever those options seem feasible. If you decide to use a Web site to attract business, you will also need to explain how that fits into your business plan.

- **Part Six of Your Business Plan — Your Organization's Management Team**

In this section, highlight your company's management team and staff, with special emphasis on their skills and how this group will ensure the company's profitability. It may include:

1. **The ownership structure of your business.** Explain whether your company is a sole proprietorship, a partnership, or a corporation and will indicate who holds what percentage of ownership in the organization.

2. **The internal management team.** List your company's managers — often in the areas of sales and marketing, administration, and production — with special emphasis on their professional skills. You may want to present this information with an organizational chart, and each manager's résumé should be included, along with yours as head of the company. You should also list their salaries and benefits, including any profit-sharing plan that will be in place. Any prevailing contracts with your management team should be included in the appendix of your business plan.

In this section, you should also outline your staffing needs in detail, along with the related costs, including salaries and workers' compensation insurance. This involves deciding whether you will need employees, independent contractors, or freelancers, and who will work onsite or offsite, on a full-time or part-time basis. Even if you do not need to hire anyone to work for you at the start, your investors will want to know that you are planning for the future and that you have established human resource policies to be applied as your business grows.

- **Part Seven of Your Business Plan — Your Operating Strategy**

At this point, you will deal with the tangible needs of your business, including its facilities and equipment. Your aim will be to show the reader what you have done up to that point related to the startup of your business and that you have a clear picture of everything that is involved in producing and distributing your product. This part of your plan involves two phases:

1. **The development stage.** Describe the manufacturing process used in producing your product, explain how it will meet industry standards and regulations, and indicate any problems that you may run into during production. In addition, list your suppliers, the agreements you will have with them, and the related quality-control measures you intend to use.

2. **The production process.** Indicate your business hours. If your business is seasonal, you will need to make that clear to your potential investors. Explain how long it will take to

produce your product, when you plan to begin production, and the equipment and materials you will need to do the job.

- **Part Eight of Your Business Plan — Your Financial Plan**

This section is a key factor in attracting investors to your business, and all of your startup expenses and regular operating expenses will be included here. Write a brief analysis of these three statements, which will be included in the appendix:

- **Your income statement.** Show your anticipated revenue, expenses, and profit for the first year of operation, by month.

- **Your cash flow projection.** Show the dollar amount that will be realized or expended during your first year of operation, by month.

- **Your balance sheet.** Summarize the information contained in the two preceding statements, clearly indicating the potential assets, liabilities, and earning for the entire year.

Tip #46: How to Give an Effective Presentation or Conduct a Training Session

When they are preparing to give a presentation or train staff, many managers find themselves using audiovisual materials to amplify their message, but they must also realize what many politicians have discovered — namely that the audience must be led to trust in them if they want to succeed. In addition, they should ask themselves if they have given the "trust factor" the attention it deserves in the past or foolishly taken it for granted.

Here are some essential factors that should be part of every business presentation:

- **Relate to your audience.** Since people sometimes have difficulty understanding ideas that are new to them, you should be prepared to clarify what you will be telling them and fill in any details the group may need, especially in regard to any key terms you may use throughout the presentation. You should always be prepared for the question-and-answer period, which should be included at the end of each session.

If your presentation is interactive, rather than one that takes the lecture approach, try to find something helpful in the comments the participants make, deal with any doubts they have about what was said (for example, the reasons that you feel profits will rise sharply in the next quarter), and indicate any areas of mutual agreement that have been reached.

The goal is to establish a certain "comfort level" with the group, and if you are sincere, your body language — your facial mannerisms and gestures — will correlate with what you are saying. This, along with preciseness in the terms you use, can prove to be a winning combination in accomplishing what you set out to do.

- **Gain the confidence of the group.** If your audience feels you are knowledgeable and dealing with them honestly, their confidence will increase, and they will also be receptive if you seem to relate well to them because of your common background or past experience. They will be particularly interested in what you have to say if you present some solutions to current or potential problems, or can suggest realistic ways of reaching goals you have in common with them.

You should also provide support and encouragement for the audience in your presentation and let participants know that you are not there to dictate to them in any way. Wise presenters take the time to rehearse what they are going to say so that they will not seem unsure of themselves and can avoid any hint of confusion among the group.

- **Use color effectively in your presentations.** Experts tell us that the dominant color in a certain setting will have an effect on the kind of communication that goes on, indicating that the décor selected for rooms where company training will be conducted should be chosen carefully and that the misuse of color can have a negative effect on the audience. In addition, the use of slides should be limited to ten to twelve.

Green and blue are considered the easiest colors to use when you are preparing graphics for such an event, and if you overdo the use of animations and sounds, the audience will become confused and unable to focus on the heart of your message. Charts, graphs, and photos should only be used to complement what you are saying, not detract from it.

- **Choose the right typefaces for your slides.** Your text will be easy to read if it contrasts well with the background (light text with a dark background), and your color scheme should be consistent throughout the presentation. Limit yourself to two fonts — preferably Times New Roman or Arial ¬— of at least 30 points so that everyone in the room can read the material, and use "bullets" to emphasize the key points you are trying to make.

- **Get positive and negative feedback from your audience.** Perhaps the best way of getting feedback after giving a presentation is to provide an anonymous questionnaire that participants can complete at the end of the session. Regardless of the form that feedback takes, pay close attention to comments that seem credible and coherent, and take notes on them that you can use when getting ready for your next session.

To conclude, you will be operating under a handicap if you fail to give the art of persuasion, your body language, the correct use of audiovisual material, and the opportunity for feedback from the audience the attention they deserve during the presentation process. Your training session will not be as smooth and complete as it could have been, and you will not accomplish everything you had planned. In the end, the message must come from you.

Tip #47: How to Network Online Effectively to Advance Your Career

While it should never be used as a substitute for other forms of social contact available, networking online has its place. When we use this casual environment, we should be just as professional, tactful, and polite as we are during a face-to-face meeting or conversation on the telephone. In addition, we should exercise extra caution, because the statements we make and the information we provide can be forwarded to others or filed away, with the source duly noted.

Here are some simple steps to follow to ensure that your networking skills prove to be a valuable tool rather than a source of embarrassment or criticism:

- **Choose the right venues for this activity.** Try to select forums that are well moderated, with participants whose interests are similar to yours, including specific business and industry sites. Note that you will only be welcome at the site if you follow the guidelines established for its use. For example, some chat rooms are strictly social and they ban any promotional activities, while other forums have "doing business" as their main purpose.

- **Include a signature line in your postings.** This block of text, which can be attached at the end of your electronic message and will identify you to the reader, should include your name, the name of your organization, and your contact information. Proofread each item to check that you are not passing along confidential information, check for errors in spelling and grammar, and check for any indication that the message was written in haste without much thought behind it. You should also ensure that nothing you have written can be misinterpreted, remembering that your reader will not have your "tone of voice" as a guideline and cannot read minds.

- **Avoid making comments that are negative or defensive in nature.** Always resist the impulse to retaliate when someone else who participates in the network is hostile or unpleasant, because doing otherwise will only cause the situation to go from bad to worse.

- **Do not imitate the pundits you watch on television.** Your postings will be well received if you comment on those topics where you are well informed and have something worthwhile to contribute to the group. There may also be times when you will decide to contact some individual participants instead of e-mailing everyone. Avoid contact members only when you need something from them. Instead, be willing to provide information to them, offer your help, or share an interesting article with someone.

Tip #48: How You Can Prepare to Do Business in a Global Economy

If you want to advance in your career, you must also know how to succeed in business on an international level. You will have to do more detailed preparation than you would if you were traveling to another part of the United States in order to "close the deal." Whether you are meeting with foreign representatives of your organization or new clients located overseas, here are some tips that will help you accomplish what you have set out to do:

- **Lay the groundwork for your trip while you are still at home.** Do some research on the business practices and social etiquette of the country you will be visiting, using the Internet and travel books as your guides. If you can, you might also want to consult with a colleague from your company who is familiar with the territory. While mastering a foreign language may not be your strong suit, try to learn some key phrases before traveling to your destination. Your host will appreciate the effort you make, and it will also help create better rapport between you and those you encounter during your visit.

Above all, here, as in virtually every situation where you interact with others, you will not go wrong by being polite, patient, and respectful. A stereotype exists that Americans are arrogant and overbearing, and you will want to counteract that image.

- **Take steps to avoid the consequences of jet lag, which may cause you to be ineffective in a meeting.** Never begin such a trip by being sleep-deprived, and set your watch to the "new" time before you leave home. If possible, get to your destination a few days before your seminar or meeting is scheduled, and allow your body to adjust to the change. To avoid dehydration, which can be caused by the dry cabin air of your plane and worsen your jet lag, drink plenty of water before, during, and after your trip, and avoid alcohol and caffeine. At the end of your flight, try not to sleep until nighttime, with the possible exception of a one-hour nap.

Conclusion

Even if you have outstanding leadership skills, you will want to become familiar with the many things managers do on a daily basis before pursuing an MBA. They often include:

- Writing a comprehensive business plan.

- Giving presentations and conducting training sessions.

- Learning to deal with today's global economy.

Chapter 5
Career Opportunities You Will Have with an MBA

If you are interested in advancing your career and want to earn a graduate degree to develop new skills, there are many reasons why attending business school may be the best choice for you.

Tip #49: What Getting Your MBA Degree Can Do for You

These are some of the positive aspects of earning your advanced degree:

1. **Some things you can accomplish in graduate school.** Once you have completed your graduate program, you will find that you have sharpened your business skills, gone further in advancing your personal and career goals, and increased your earning power. A business degree can help you build your career and realize your goals in almost any organization, large, small, or in between.

People with an MBA can be found in nonprofit organizations, the military, government, the healthcare field, and consulting among other industries. Some business school graduates even decide to start their own company or run a small family business they have inherited, because they know that versatility and applicability are two of a business degree's best characteristics.

2. **What your MBA program will be like.** You may be surprised to know that the typical MBA curriculum offers a balance of a wide variety of courses, all of which are geared toward helping students think analytically while building on their quantitative skills. Some of the courses involve mathematics, and if you are not confident about your current math skills, you may want to take some courses to review the basics at a local community college before enrolling in business school.

3. **What is involved in applying for admission to graduate school.** When you are ready to take this step, your goal will be to convince the admissions officer that you can succeed, both academically and professionally, at their institution. You will need to have a clear picture of your career goals and abilities to determine if this specialty is right for you and select the graduate school you want to attend.

4. **What to do after you have made your decision.** Here are some tips for you to follow once you have decided to apply:

   - Speak candidly to admissions officers about why you are seeking an advanced degree, explain your goals and ambitions, and discuss your reasons for selecting that particular graduate school and program.

   - Be certain that your career goals are based on a realistic analysis of your past work experience and your skills and training, and that you meet all the academic admissions requirements of that school. No matter where you apply, you will be able to enhance your skills in accounting, marketing, finance, economics, organization design, statistics, policy, and operations through your coursework.

- When you have your admissions interview, make it clear that you hope to contribute something worthwhile to the academic community once you begin your program, that you are familiar with the school, and that you feel you and the school are compatible.

5. **Consider the role played by each graduate school's culture in making your decision.** Be aware that business school cultures vary, just as industry and corporate cultures do, and you may want to speak to some current and former students to gain knowledge in this area before proceeding further with your application. For your own well-being, it is essential that your personality and your chosen school's environment blend together well. Every graduate program has its strong points, content, and boundaries for you to consider as you make your choice.

Tip #50: For the Female Student — Removing the Mystery from Getting an MBA

Today, about 40 percent of those who take the GMAT test are women, and many graduate schools would like to see more qualified female applicants pursue an MBA degree.

Unfortunately, a number of common misconceptions still prevent some women — along with other worthwhile candidates — from taking that step.

If your misgivings are as strong as your desire to pursue a graduate degree and you are having trouble making a decision, here are some facts that should interest any serious business school candidate, male or female:

- Business schools vary widely, and some of them are more focused on attracting and supporting women in their MBA program than others. They are also aware that female students are more likely than their male counterparts to seek out an academic environment where they will meet people with backgrounds and life experiences similar to their own. Women tend to approach their graduate studies from a somewhat different perspective than men do.

- When women research business schools, they should look at the percentage of women enrolled in the current MBA class and the quantity and variety of women's organizations on campus, along with the percentage of women on the faculty and the number of women who have been invited to speak on campus recently. They should also investigate any scholarships and financial aid packages that may be targeted toward female graduate students who attend the school.

Tip #51: For the Minority Student — What You Need to Know to Succeed

Business schools throughout the United States want to provide their students with a diversified environment, and they have become associated with many outreach groups that offer seminars, informational sessions, fellowships, and scholarships especially created for minority students in order to attract them. Here is the situation that exists today:

1. **Increasing the representation of Hispanic students in business schools.** The American Assembly of Collegiate Schools of Business reports that less than 2 percent of business school faculty members are Hispanic, and only 5 percent of the MBA students in this country are Hispanic. Given this, minority young people often question how they can possibly aspire to a career in management if mentors they can relate to are a rare commodity and financial aid for their studies is lacking at the graduate level.

To add a positive note in this regard, the Consortium for Graduate Study in Management at **http://www.cgsm.org/about/index.asp** assists students by awarding more than 350 fellowships specifically to minority students every year. The National Black MBA Association at **http://www.nbmbaa.org** also provides scholarships. In addition, the most serious problem in regard to the under-representation of minority students in MBA programs seems to be that many of those who would do well in business school are unaware of what acquiring an advanced degree could do for their careers and their income in the future.

2. **What minority business students need to remember.** People in this category need to see that a graduate degree will improve their chance for success and provide them with training that will open doors for them in the business world — if they are willing to take the time and make the

effort entailed in earning that degree. At the same time, American business schools consider Native Americans (including U.S. Pacific Islanders), African Americans, and Hispanic Americans to be under-represented in their MBA programs. If you belong to one of these groups and want to change that pattern, you need to set about the task of making yourself known to these institutions; the results may pleasantly surprise you.

3. **Take advantage of the mentoring opportunities available to you.** This may be what you need to increase your overall business awareness and prepare for the day when you apply to business school. Management Leadership for Tomorrow (MLT) at **http://www.ml4t.org**, for example, is a program that has successfully matched 350 minority students with experienced business professionals who act as their mentors.

4. **It is also important to do your own research** — Besides visiting the Web site of an accredited school that interests you, note that open-house weekends, minority receptions, and similar events will give you an opportunity to interact with instructors, students, and future applicants as you research business schools. You can also gather information about the clubs and programs available to provide the support you will need.

5. **Use resources that will help you find the school that is right for you** — As you search for a graduate program that meets your needs and expectations, you can visit the Advanced Business School Search online at **http://www. princetonreview.com/mba/research/advsearch/match.asp** to view the demographics that indicate the percentage of

minorities, women, and international students enrolled at the individual schools listed. You can use the links provided to visit the schools' individual Web sites for additional information. You can also become part of an institution's student recruitment process if you indicate that you want them to contact you, which can be done while you are submitting an online application or visiting their Web site.

Tip #52: For the International Student — What You Need to Know to Succeed

Once you have made the decision to pursue an advanced degree in the United States, you will have many other decisions to make and many questions to answer before you apply to business school. What follows are some essential points to consider as you take this step:

1. **Decide where you want to study for your MBA.** Because the country is so large, you will have many options in regard to where enroll in business school. At the same time, you should look for an institution that offers you a good MBA program that is affordable, and you will need to determine if you prefer living in a large city or a small college town, and what type of climate you are used to. Because of America's size, where you decide to attend school will have an impact on how convenient it will be for you to return to your home country for emergencies, holidays, or a vacation.

2. **Know why choosing the right location is important.** Here are some points you should remember as you decide where to attend business school in the United States:

- If you settle in a big city, its vastness and fast-paced atmosphere may seem overwhelming at first, and the cost of living may be high. At the same time, you may find it easier to become familiar with and adapt to the American way of life in this kind of environment, which offers many cultural advantages, and you are also more likely to meet other students who are in the same situation.

- If you settle in a smaller town, you will be able to adjust to your unfamiliar surrounding more gradually, feel less overwhelmed by what is going on around you, and find it easier to control your living expenses.

There are advantages to living in either locale, but taking the step of coming to America to earn your MBA involves preparing ahead of time for your new venture.

3. **Determine the number of international students who attend the school that interests you.** You should not base your final decision on this factor alone, but it is certainly one that you will not want to overlook. If a large number of foreign students are enrolled there, the administration should be more aware of their needs and the difficulties they face than other schools might be, and while such a situation is not necessary, it could prove helpful as you go through graduate school.

4. **Decide if you can afford to attend graduate school at this time.** In America, advanced study is not automatically supplemented by the government, and even though some scholarships are available to graduate students, going to

business school here may be more expensive than it would be in your home country.

Do some research to see if you qualify for a scholarship, which may be provided by your government, the United States federal government, or a religious organization. These scholarships may include stipends that help students maintain an acceptable quality of life as they complete their course of study.

5. **Discover another way to finance your education.** In addition to the scholarships offered to you, the school where you plan to enroll may have some work-study choices available that interest you. Such a program involves working on campus in some capacity or teaching introductory-level courses to undergraduates and can offset some of the expense entailed in going to graduate school.

6. **Know the requirements when you apply to business school as a foreign student.** For your American counterparts, the application process to be accepted as a graduate student, which includes registering for the GRE and GMAT exams, is fairly complicated. Also, in the United States, standardized test centers tend to fill up quickly. You should register early and take the required tests as soon possible. This will ensure that your test scores will be received at the graduate school of your choice in a timely manner as you complete your application.

As a foreign student, you will find there are even more procedures for you to follow, since you will have to complete the steps for maintaining legal student status while you are in the United States and take the required standardized tests in your own country as well. However, if you organize all the documents you need to complete your application and schedule their submission correctly by allowing ample time for them to reach their destination, you will avoid many problems and personal anxiety.

7. **Gather the documents you will need before coming to America.** When you leave your home country, you will need to acquire a student visa (Category F-1) at the U.S. consulate office 120 days or less before your classes are scheduled to begin, and you will need a passport that is valid for at least six months from the date of that visit. You must also bring the following items with you:

   - A Student Exchange Visitor Information System (SEVIS)–generated form I-20, issued by the institution you plan to attend, which cannot be changed once the form is presented. This information must also be approved by the U.S. Department of Homeland Security (DHS).

   - Visa Forms DS-156 and DS-158 (and DS-157, if required), along with a two-inch by two-inch color photograph, your graduation certificate, your undergraduate transcript, your Grade Point Average (GPA) certificate, and your scores from the GRE and Test of English as a Foreign Language (TOEFL®) exams.

8. **Take the TOEFL test when you apply as a foreign student.** If English is your second language, many schools will also want you to take the TOEFL test to ensure that you are proficient in standard English and will be able to

function in an academic environment where that language predominates. This requirement applies to international students who plan to study in America or Canada, and to other institutions throughout the world where classes are conducted in English.

9. **Prepare for the TOEFL exam.** To practice for this test, you can use the TOEFL Test Preparation Kit, available from Educational Testing Service (ETS) at www.ets.org, which contains a book, a CD-ROM, and four audio CDs. This special prep kit includes 14 hours of practice items, with 980 questions from previous exams and 5 practice tests.

10. **Know what to expect when you take the TOEFL exam.** In most countries, you will find that the test is computer-based, and it will include tutorials for reviewing basic computer skills, such as scrolling and using a mouse, and the right way to use the testing tools located on the computer screen. As each section of the test begins, a tutorial will demonstrate how you should answer the questions that follow and will provide some practice questions; those items will not be timed.

11. **Realize what the TOEFL® test is like.** This exam, which is based on standard North American English, is divided into the following four sections:

    - **Listening.** This section evaluates the student's skill in understanding spoken English by having them use headphones and listen to taped talks and conversations and then answer about 50 related questions within the allotted time of 60 minutes.

- **Structure.** This section tests the student's skill in recognizing correct grammar in standard written English within 15 or 20 minutes, and it includes 20 or 25 questions.

These first two sections of the test are computer-adaptive, which means that questions you are given to answer will be determined by whether you answer each item correctly, which will be referred to as your "performance level." Note that once you click the "Confirm Answer" button as you respond to a question, you will not be able to go back and change your answer.

- **Reading.** This section evaluates the student's skill in reading and comprehending brief passages typical of those used in North American colleges and universities. The time allotted for this, which depends on the number of questions the section contains, may be as much as 90 minutes, and this timing will be clearly indicated on your computer screen.

- **Writing.** This section evaluates the student's skill in writing in English, and the system assigns a topic taken from those listed in the "TOEFL Information Bulletin." Using grammar that is both clear and correct, you will be expected to comment on the topic provided and include relevant examples or evidence. You will have 30 minutes to do this.

12. **Understand your score on the TOEFL test.** Your final score on this test will categorize your English proficiency level as elementary, intermediate, working, or advanced, and

you should verify the minimum score requirement at the business school you plan to attend when you apply.

Your total score for the exam may range from 0 to 100, and it is a combination of your scores on each of the four separate sections, which are scored on a range from 0 to 30. For additional information about this test, visit the TOEFL Web site at **www. TOEFL.org**, where you can practice online, or contact The Princeton Review by calling 800-2Review (800-273-8439).

13. **Adjust to the culture while you study in the United States.** Although you do not want to lose your identity or pretend to be someone you are not, your adjustment to living in the United States will be easier if you are open to the way in which things are done here, including our casual attitude toward mealtime, and adjust your daily routine. Once you are settled here, you may want to invite a new friend to your home for what you consider to be a traditional dinner and experience the enjoyment of sharing your culture with someone in this country for the first time.

14. **Learn to find time for yourself while you are in business school.** While you will spend a lot of time attending classes, studying, and completing your assignments, you also need balance in your life in order to reach your goal. You can do this by exploring the city or town in which you live, joining organizations on campus or in your local community, or taking part in any worthwhile activity that will provide some "real-world" experience to complement your academic studies. Far from being a waste of time, doing this will replenish your inner resources and aid in your personal development.

Conclusion

There is no doubt that earning an MBA can increase your earning power and help you realize your career goals, but before you apply to any business school, you may want to research the following factors:

- What your graduate program will be like and how to apply.

- How to answer your special concerns if you are a female student.

- The information minority students need.

- The information international students need.

CHAPTER 6
FINDING MONEY TO PAY FOR YOUR MBA DEGREE

Since you will be investing time and money to earn your graduate degree, you will also want to spend some time thinking about what the return on that investment will be. After weighing the intangibles, such as your goals and your career satisfaction, consider the financial consequences of your decision. About 70 percent of the students in an MBA program receive some kind of financial aid, and you will need to decide if you are ready to assume such a sizable debt, keeping in mind the financial obligations you already have.

Two conflicting theories are at work when someone is deciding if the time is financially right to invest money in a graduate degree. With the cyclical argument, we are told it is best to enroll when the economy is robust and the unemployment rate is low. The countercyclical argument tells us to enroll when the economy is in a downturn to sharpen our skills and be prepared for the upswing in job growth and availability that is sure to follow . In the end, you will find yourself applying to business school when the time seems right for you.

Tip #53: Financial Factors to Consider

Once you calculate the cost of attending graduate school, find out how much financial aid you will be able to obtain and what part of that financial aid will consist of a loan requiring no collateral, and then determine how you are going to repay it. In addition, you should keep the following financial factors in mind in reaching your decision:

- The size and the prevailing interest rate of the student loan you take out

- Your relocation costs and the accompanying changes in your living expenses (if applicable)

- Whether, in your particular circumstances, it would be more costly for you to be a part-time or full-time student when you weigh all the factors involved

As a rule, the sooner you earn an MBA degree, the sooner your potential earning power will increase; conversely, if you study on a part-time basis, the cost of getting your MBA will be spread out over a longer period of time, which may also be to your advantage. The choice you make should be based solidly on your particular circumstances.

Tip #54: Your Eligibility for Financial Aid when You Are in Business School

Once you have been admitted into its MBA program, your school will compile a financial aid package for you. This is often a combination of merit-based and need-based assistance. The merit-based portion will focus on your academic record, your personal achievements, your work experience, and other related factors. Your eligibility for need-based financial aid will focus on your financial status when compared with the actual cost of obtaining your advanced degree. Here are some factors to consider:

1. **Calculating the cost of getting your MBA.** The total cost of your graduate school education, which the school will determine, may be based on a leaner budget than the one you have in mind, and you will be expected to adjust your lifestyle accordingly to participate in the financial aid program. Any consumer debt you have already assumed will not be factored into this budget. Graduate students are thought to be "independent adults" who are self-supporting rather than dependent on their parents' income. If you are married, your spouse's income will also be considered in formulating this budget, along with any assets you may have.

2. **Applying for need-based financial aid (if applicable).** In this case, you will have to file one or more need-analysis forms, and they will be used to determine what you can contribute toward the cost of your education. All federal student aid programs require that you file a Free Application for Federal Student Aid (FAFSA), and you will need to reapply for financial aid each year you want to receive it, which will be a special concern for those who want to participate in a two-year MBA program.

Your business school will have hard copies of the FAFSA form available, and the financial aid office will help you in completing the application process. You can also apply online at **http://www.fafsa.ed.gov**. This method is quicker and less difficult to complete than the offline procedure. The Help section at this Web site will guide you as you fill out the form, and the business school you list on the application will also receive your information in a timely manner.

Regardless of how you apply for financial aid, you will need to compile all the required documentation indicated and fill out the form accurately and completely to obtain a loan. If you have any difficulty in doing this and you cannot find the solution to your problem by referring to the information posted on the Web site, you can call 1-800-4-FED-AID (1-800-433-3243) for assistance.

3. **Negotiating your student loan with a Financial Aid Officer (FAO).** Be aware that the initial financial aid offer you receive may seem insufficient to you, because it may be made with the expectation that you will ask to increase it. If you feel a genuine need for additional funds to cover your expenses while you are studying, there is no harm in seeing if you can do just that.

If you decide to take this step, be polite, firm, and reasonable during your negotiations with the FAO. To make your point, be prepared to explain why you need the additional funds and why you feel justified in asking for a student loan that is larger than the one being offered to you.

4. **Knowing how your student loan will be handled —** Ordinarily, your business school will verify your eligibility for the loan, but a bank or some other financial institution may lend you the money, and that institution will need to approve you as a good credit risk for them. Following standard procedure, your lender will examine the amount of debt you have already assumed and your payment history. Also, certain schools may ask you for supplemental

documentation, including your most recent income tax form, as a prerequisite for providing any financial aid to you.

Tip #55: What You Should Do Before You Apply for a Student Loan

Before requesting a loan as part of the financial aid package offered by your school, you should take the following steps:

- Ask for your credit rating and your credit score from Equifax, Experian, and TransUnion, the three major credit-reporting agencies, and have any errors you may find on their reports corrected. These two items make up what is known as your credit profile, and any consumer debt you have when you apply for a student loan will not be deferred while you are working toward your MBA. Clearly, taking out a student loan means that you will be assuming a new financial obligation in addition to the ones you already have.

- Note also that, as is the case when you want to obtain a mortgage or car loan, the less available credit you have, the more likely it is you will obtain the loan you are seeking. At the same time, you should have sufficient funds to allow for emergencies; many financially savvy adults accomplish this by keeping the equivalent of three to six months' salary in a savings account.

Tip #56: What You Should Know About Getting a Major Loan of Any Kind

To succeed in getting a student loan, you will have to meet

some basic requirements, such as earning a certain minimum income. In addition, other factors may work in your favor when you apply, including the following:

- You have been living at your current address for at least two years.

- You are a home owner rather than a renter. This indicates that you have accumulated equity in that property.

- You have a checking account, a savings account, or a bank credit card that you have paid on time according to the lender's standards.

If you are self-employed and feel this may prove to be an obstacle when you are looking for a loan, you can be proactive and determine if your potential lender needs any additional information to ensure that your application will be accepted.

If you are not already in the habit of doing so periodically, request your credit report from TransUnion, Equifax, and Experian; look for any errors they might contain; and doing this yourself will not have a negative effect on your credit rating. The Fair Credit Reporting Act gives you the right to question anything in your credit report that you consider to be false or incomplete.

As you examine these reports, look for charges and any other information that does not belong there. In addition, keep the following in mind:

- If there are any negative items on your report, such as a charge-off that has now expired and should have been removed, contact the Dispute Investigation Department of TransUnion or Equifax by certified mail to have that error corrected. (Experian requires that such requests be made online.)

- If you discover that an account you know is "closed" is identified as being "open" on your report, you can dispute that. Whenever you close an account in the future, ask that creditor to earmark that account as being "closed by the consumer" to avoid any negative consequences.

- If you contact a credit bureau, include copies of written documentation and pertinent information to support your claim and prove that it is valid. Current law states that the credit bureau in question must complete their investigation of the matter and correct your report within 30 days and notify you of their action. At times, you may solve the problem more easily by dealing with the creditor that submitted the erroneous information. Their authority carries more weight than yours as an individual, and they can notify all three credit bureaus for you once the correction is made.

By way of encouragement, authorities tell us that 75 percent of all MBA students also hold jobs, including 61 percent who work full time, and shuttling between the world of work and the world of academia is far from uncommon for them. In addition, many students feel that these two environments reinforce each other, and you are far less likely to run into any major problems while you are in graduate school if you have your financial affairs in order before your classes begin.

Tip #57: Private Student Loan Sources That May Be Available to You

In addition to Sallie Mae, which may be referenced in the Distance Learning section of this book, the following organizations are considered top sources for securing a loan to finance a student's graduate school education:

- Nellie Mae EXCEL Grad Loan (call 1-800-FOR TUITION) at **www.nelliemae.com**

- The Access Group (call 1-800-282-1550) at **www. accessgroup.org**

- The Education Resources Group (call 1-800-255-TERI) at **www.educationresourcesgroup.org**

- Citibank (call 1-800-967-2400) at **https://studentloan. citibank.com/s/slcsite**

Employer Tuition Benefits for Business School May Also Be Available to You

Before you decide to obtain a student loan from any of the sources already mentioned, think about what you plan to do with your MBA and what your company's expectations of you are. Some employers will expect you to reimburse them if you leave the company once you have your degree, and, for ethical reasons, certain schools will not permit you to use the services of their placement office if you are being sponsored by your employer.

You should know if you will be reimbursed for tuition only or if your company will pay for all your educational expenses. In some cases, they may only pay for those courses you complete with a certain required grade or for the student loans you have already taken out. When it comes to determining the educational benefits that are available to you, your employer's human resources department should be able to provide all the information you need.

Tip #58: What Getting an Internship Can Do for You as You Earn Your MBA

If you are in a two-year graduate program, you will be given an opportunity to apply your skills to the business world as an MBA intern between your first and second year in the program. Many companies do most of their hiring from such internship candidate pools, and this experience is a valuable part of any business school's program. Since this opportunity is so important in advancing your career, you may want to start planning for it before your courses begin. Anyone who is part of your professional network may be able to guide you in the right direction. Here are some points for you to consider:

1. **Do not hesitate to take the initiative in becoming an intern.** If you find a location where you would like to function as an intern, but the exact position you are looking for does not exist, you can try to play a role in creating it. To accomplish this, submit your résumé, request an interview, and then lobby enthusiastically for the job. You may be pleasantly

surprised at the results, because internships are intended to end with an offer for a long-term position for those who show that they deserve it.

2. **Find out what will be expected of you in this capacity.** You will soon discover that your internship has a definite job description that is clear to your employer and to the other members of the staff, if it is worthwhile. Your supervisor, who will also be your mentor in an ideal situation, should set the tone here, and your progress on the job should also be monitored if you are to gain any benefit from the experience. Dress and act professionally, and try to maintain a positive attitude despite any stress you may feel because of work and school obligations.

3. **Approach the job of intern with the right attitude.** At the same time, show your interest in the organization and the industry it represents, be congenial with other employees, and prove your competence by doing the basic tasks that are assigned to you well and with enthusiasm. This is the only way those in authority will be able to determine that you would be an asset to the organization in a permanent position and that you will be able to take on additional responsibilities at the appropriate time. Do not hesitate to ask questions, to learn, and to participate in new projects as they come along.

Tip #59: Another Possibility to Consider — Funding Your Education as a Graduate Teaching Assistant

Graduate teaching assistants often receive a stipend from their school that ranges from $6,500 to $15,000 per year, along with free tuition. Depending on the institution's policy, teaching assistants may be eligible for other benefits as well, along with gaining practical experience when they assume this role. This is what being a graduate assistant entails:

1. **What you will be required to do in this position** — The tasks you will be expected to perform as a graduate teaching assistant may include one or more of the following:

    - Teaching or assisting an instructor with one or more college courses.

    - Grading the term papers and tests of undergraduate students.

    - Maintaining regular office hours and meeting with those students.

    - Conducting laboratory sessions and "study and review" sessions with those students.

2. **What your work schedule will be like in this situation** — Graduate teaching assistants are expected to work about 20 hours each week. In addition to having a manageable work schedule, you will find you are doing a job that is funding your education and helping you to prepare for your future career because of the exposure it gives you on a daily basis.

Tip #60: Using Scholarships, Grants, and Fellowships to Finance Business School

Any funds that fall into one of these categories do not have to be repaid, and graduate schools sometimes award them to MBA candidates based on the applicant's GRE and specialty test scores, financial hardship, and other factors. Along with covering the expense of tuition and supplies, these awards, which vary in amount, may include a stipend for the student's living expenses.

The awarding of scholarships is based on a student's scholastic ability, a particular talent that student may have, or certain other related factors. You can find out more about scholarships by consulting with your school's financial aid office or going to that school's Web site, and you can also visit the online funding databases, such as **www.fastweb.com**, **www.findtuition.com/scholarships**, or FinAid at **www.finaid.org**.

Conclusion

While finding money to pay for your graduate courses may not be easy, it is also far from impossible. Here are some points for you to consider:

- Your eligibility for financial aid.

- The right way of getting a student loan.

- Private student loan sources you can use.

- Employer tuition reimbursement.

- Completing an internship or graduate teaching assistantship.

- Obtaining a scholarship, grant, or fellowship.

CHAPTER 7
WHAT IS INVOLVED IN GETTING INTO BUSINESS SCHOOL

Undergraduate course requirements may vary from one business school to another, and having some background in the field of calculus, statistics, or economics will be in your favor. Once you decide to apply, you should contact your undergraduate school to determine their procedure and timeliness in forwarding transcripts of your grades when you request them, and work from there.

Tip #61: How Your Undergraduate Record Can Affect Your Admission

When your transcripts are forwarded, the business school in question will take the following two factors into consideration:

- The undergraduate school you attended, the difficulty of the courses in your undergraduate program, and the competition you faced there as an undergraduate student.

- Your undergraduate grade point average (GPA), with special emphasis on your main area of study and any significant fluctuations in your GPA from one semester to another. Often, they will consider your overall GPA along with courses that are relevant to their program.

Admissions officers consider your GPA to be a long-term indicator of how well you will perform as a graduate student because it tells them how motivated you are and it measures the consistency of your academic work. Most business schools require a minimum GPA of 3.0 or 3.3 for admitting students into their program.

Tip #62: What You Should Know About the Standardized Tests You Will Take

Applicants to any business school come from a variety of backgrounds, and the reputation of the school where they received their earlier training is not always known. This means that college officials use these tests to gauge the ability of those who want to be accepted into their graduate program in a reliable way, particularly their skill in dealing with unfamiliar situations. In addition, you will be expected to read and summarize a large amount of material within a relatively brief time.

Here are some common factors found in standardized tests like the GRE and the GMAT that you will want to remember:

- **These test scores are based on percentiles.** This means that rather than being related to some well-established "perfect score," your performance will be evaluated according to what everyone else in the group being tested accomplished on the day of the exam. In addition, since these exams are corrected by a computer, there is no concern as to how you arrived at your answer; the only issue here is whether that response is right or wrong. This is the situation you will face on test day for both the GRE and the GMAT. You will be free to use alternative methods to arrive at your conclusions, but you should also be aware that you will be give full credit or no credit for every response, and the test will be timed.

- **Try to use strategy as you take these tests.** Each correct response is of equal value. You will not want to answer an "easy" question incorrectly because you acted hastily and thought you needed to spend more time for the "hard" ones. A correct answer will never contain information that is not found in the passage you have read, but it will match the author's tone. At the same time, those who make up the test find ways to disguise what they are testing, and they sometimes use "trick" responses that may seem to be correct but contain errors in reasoning, which you should be able to detect if you have prepared properly.

- **The essay questions can present a special challenge.** Your main objective here will be to ensure that your response to these items is clear, definite, and well organized. This means you should support the stand you take in your argument by providing concrete examples from your past experience, current events, history, or any other relevant source that comes to mind, and use them to form the foundation for your thesis.

Tip #63: What You Should Know if You Decide to Apply to Business School

1. **Beginning your search to find the right school.** In deciding where to apply for your MBA, you should gather information from a variety of sources. You can begin by discussing this with faculty members at your undergraduate school who seem to share your academic and research interests. When you do this, you may find that your professors have colleagues who teach at other graduate schools, and these people may also be able to help you in reaching your decision.

2. **Choosing a location that will suit your needs.** If you are used to living in an urban setting, you may want to avoid business schools located in a rural area; if you prefer a temperate climate, you may want to concentrate your search on schools located in the southern states. About nine months before you plan to begin classes, you should register for any courses that are prerequisites or that you know are needed to supplement your academic background.

3. **Researching various graduate school programs.** The print and electronic materials provided by graduate schools contain the most accurate information you will find about the programs themselves, the services available on campus, the prevailing school culture, the composition of the faculty, and the current student body. They will also tell you what

the school is looking for in its potential students and how you can apply for admission.

Referencing media guidebooks can also be helpful in doing your research, but they are not the only source of information you will need, and they certainly are not the most important one. Many books are available on studying for an MBA and furthering your career, and they will provide valuable information as you continue your search.

4. **Taking the next step in applying to graduate school.** When you come across a program that seems interesting to you, follow the instructions provided on that school's Web site for obtaining further information, and then automatically enter an "inquiry for additional information" on their database. As you review the results of your search, focus on the school's GPA and undergraduate course requirements and the years of work experience that are the established standard there. In the end, your chances of being admitted will be based on the quality of your application rather than on some impressive, arbitrary average that is being touted on the Web site, such as "only one out of every four applicants is accepted into our program."

5. **Making sure that the school is accredited.** Along with ensuring the accreditation of the *institution* you plan to attend, it will interest you to know that the Association to Advance Collegiate Schools of Business (AACSB) gives accreditation to business departments. To earn it, the programs and faculties of those schools must meet the standards established by the association. This will not be a concern if you plan to start your own business or if your employer accepts a degree from a local business school

without such accreditation, but these two situations are the exception rather than the rule.

6. **Knowing where the current MBA school rankings may fit in your research.** Although they are widely used, graduate school rankings or comparisons of business school programs are quite arbitrary if all those schools are accredited. Much depends on the publication releasing their study's findings, the manner in which research about the schools listed is conducted, and the way in which the resulting statistics are interpreted. Due to the varied criteria used in rating these programs, some worthwhile graduate schools can be excluded from the rankings unfairly, especially if the student body happens to be small.

7. **Successfully dealing with your business school's placement office.** Any published salary statistics will help you assess the alumni job placement success rate of a school that interests you. This is also an indication of how the rest of the world rates MBAs who graduate from that institution. In the real world, there is no such thing as 100 percent job placement of any graduating class because of constant fluctuations in the job market.

There may also be a difference — positive or negative —¬ between the current job market and the one you will have to face after receiving your MBA. At the same time, it is unlikely that you will ever regret taking the time to attend graduate school and preparing to advance as a manager.

8. **Knowing how admissions officers will view your application.** Business schools use the application process to assess who you are at this point in your life and why

you want to take the step of pursuing an advanced degree. You should be prepared to use every part of the process to stress your accomplishments, your team experience up to that point, and your leadership skills. The typical applicant has four to ten years of relevant work experience, and you will need to explain that you want to obtain your MBA at that point in your life for all the right reasons.

9. **Remembering what the business schools want to know.** Because admissions officers are human beings rather than computers or calculators, there is no magic formula for getting into the business school of your choice. Every application is weighed on its own merits, and certain intangible factors play a role here, along with the applicant's college transcripts and entrance test results. As part of this process, admissions officers want to make certain that the following statements are true:

   - Their program will meet your educational needs and you will blend in well with the students and faculty who make up their business school community.

   - Your interest in completing the program and earning an MBA degree is high.

   - You have set realistic goals concerning your career as a manager, and those goals are in line with the established functions of the school's placement office.

If you are certain all three factors apply in your case, you will have a distinct advantage over the competition if you can also indicate clearly where you want to go in your career and exactly how you want to get there. To accomplish this, you may want to consider visiting **http://www.careerleader.com**, a widely used self-assessment tool that may be helpful when writing your admissions essay, before you proceed any further with your application to business school.

10. **Writing a "statement of purpose" before you apply to business school.** While your business school may not require one, completing a "statement of purpose" on your own should prove enlightening, and it will also help you deal successfully with any admissions interviews or job interviews that may be in store for you in the future. Here are some tips to follow as you do it:

- Admissions officers are mainly interested in what area of research interests you as you head for graduate school. You should not attempt to explain why this is so unless your discussion is brief and has a direct relationship to those interests. In addition, do not express yourself in vague, imprecise terms. For example, instead of saying that you "want to learn more about today's global economy," indicate that you would like to research "the effect outsourcing has on manufacturing in America."

- Show that you have no preconceived ideas about your interests by using terms like "indicate" or "prove." Instead, think about "exploring" and "examining" those topics in order to discover the truth — regardless of where the road may lead you — as your goal. In addition, if you can relate what you have to say to the business school's graduate program, your explanation will carry even more weight.

11. **Allowing for the expense involved in applying to various business schools.** There will be certain incidental costs as you search for the right graduate school. With this in mind, you should narrow down your "wish list" of choices before you take any formal steps to apply, since they can also mount up significantly. These various expenses may include test-related items, registration fees, fees for transcript requests, long-distance phone calls, mailing, shipping and travel, and the application fee itself.

12. **Beginning the application process.** At the start of your search, whether you are interested in the *case-method approach* to learning, where student input is the central activity in class, or the *lecture approach*, where the instructor imparts the subject matter to students, you can visit various graduate school Web sites to obtain valuable information about them. In addition, publications like *Business Week* and *The Wall Street Journal* put out special editions devoted to the topic of business schools, which should also be helpful in making your decision about where to apply.

13. **Fine-tuning your search for the right business school.** In the course of your search, you may want to speak to people who have taken part in the graduate programs at schools that interest you. An informal interview with someone in that category may even lead to a formal recommendation, which you will need as part of your application. Since these individuals have firsthand academic experience, they can also steer you away from MBA programs and instructors that you will want to avoid. If you consult the Princeton Review's publication, *The Best 290 Business Schools,* you will find these schools'

median GPAs and GMAT scores, and you can use them to determine if you measure up to a particular institution's standards for admission.

From your perspective, the actual application process is a lengthy one and you should only consider those graduate schools where you know that earning your advanced degree would be a worthwhile experience, rather than a waste of your time and money.

14. **Other factors that may affect your decision about getting your MBA.** Here are additional points to consider as you go about searching for the business school that is right for you:

- **Research funding may be available from a business school that interests you** — While this will play a role in your decision, it should not be your only consideration. You also need to determine the cost of living in the area where the school is located — if you are unfamiliar with it — and that can vary throughout the United States, the quality of its MBA program, and its overall reputation.

- **Use background information about the school in making your decision.** The institution's reputation, basic statistics, and demographics should be of particular interest to you, but you should know more than the information that can be found on its Web site or in the catalog you receive in the mail. By going a bit further, you can detect any serious problems the school may be dealing with, such as any lawsuits that have been filed against it. You can also form a more complete picture of what life there will be like for you by doing some research online and talking to current graduate students or alumni who went through their MBA program.

A business school's reputation is especially important, because having an MBA degree from a highly rated institution will mean more than one from a lesser-known school. Also, after you graduate, you will have more opportunities and options open to you as you strive to advance your career because of its prestige.

15. **Apply to business school six months before your courses are scheduled to begin.** Once you are certain you are ready to begin working on your MBA, you will find that applying early is a wise idea. Your application will be more likely to receive the time and attention it deserves, and you will demonstrate that you are used to planning ahead and are serious about your intentions to complete the course of study offered by the school.

16. **Be sure that your application does what you want it to do.** The application is a tool for marketing yourself. You should stress your skills, your academic and work experience, and strong points of your personality in your essay. In doing this, you will give admissions officers a clear picture of your reasons for applying to graduate school. You can also show them how well you would fit into their program. Admission decisions are done in three rounds by most graduate schools, and they take place in early January, late March, and early May.

17. **Add these final touches to your application to make it complete.** You can also take the following steps to ensure that

you will be submitting an impressive, effective application that will catch the attention of admissions officers:

- Make certain that your application is complete, professional-looking, and done exactly according to the instructions you received from the school.

- Double-check your work before submitting the required items as an indication of your professionalism and your suitability as a candidate for admission to their program.

Tip #64: A Book to Help You in Your Search for the Right Business School

Best 290 Business Schools, from Princeton Review, contains valuable information on applying and being admitted to business school and funding graduate study. The book also includes a two-page write-up for each of the institutions mentioned in it. To gather the information they needed, The Princeton Review surveyed 19,000 MBA candidates throughout the United States concerning various academic issues, student life at their school, and their career opportunities.

It may interest you to know that this book also lists the top ten business schools in each of the eleven categories that follow:

- Toughest to Get Into.

- Best Classroom Experience.

- Best Career Prospects.

- Best Professors.

- Most Competitive Students.

- Most Family-Friendly.

- Best Campus Environment.

- Best Campus Facilities.

- Best Administered.

- Greatest Opportunity for Minority Students.

- Greatest Opportunity for Women.

Tip #65: When You Feel That You Want to Get into a Highly Rated MBA Program

If you are intent on doing this and have worked out the other factors involved, including financing your education and the possibility of having to relocate to enroll, you can take the following steps as you apply to one of the top business schools:

- Refine your application package in such a way that the admissions committee will easily discern what you have to bring to the MBA program and what you hope to get out of it.

- At your admissions interview, try to be fully prepared to discuss your reasons for wanting an advanced degree, why you are applying at this particular time, your personal goals, and your past accomplishments.

- In your admissions essay, show that you have researched the school thoroughly, know yourself well, and are a good "fit" for their MBA program.

Tip #66: Some Outstanding American Business Schools That May Interest You

The schools listed below are considered among those offering the finest MBA programs in the United States:

- **Harvard Business School.** Since this school uses the case method, their interactive approach combines the reality of the business world with their students' academic experience. In addition, faculty members who participate in this program work with several organizations to keep their curriculum current by completing more than 350 case studies every year.

- **Wharton Business School at the University of Pennsylvania.** This school is well known for its advanced teaching methods, the vast scope of its MBA program, and the expertise of its faculty.

- **The Kellogg School of Management at Northwestern University.** With the participation of its students, this school constantly updates its curriculum to keep up with the many changes taking place in today's business world and our global economy. In addition, since it is guided by a "learn by doing" philosophy, Kellogg provides authentic field experience for those participating in their MBA program.

- **Stanford Graduate School of Business.** Both here and abroad, this business school is considered an excellent training ground for future MBAs. Its graduate program places its emphasis on leadership, social innovation, entrepreneurship, and global awareness, which it considers essential elements of management training and career preparation.

- **The Ross School of Business at the University of Michigan.** Ross has an international reputation for excellence, and its MBA program stresses general management preparation. It also includes advanced elective courses to accommodate the individual student's needs and preferences.

Tip #67: Books That Can Guide You Through the Admissions Maze

The books listed below should prove especially helpful when you are going through the application process for business school and trying to find the right program for you:

- *Graduate School: Winning Strategies for Getting In* — This book contains a comprehensive overview of what graduate study is like, what the schools are looking for in an applicant, what makes up the complete application package, selecting a program, improving your chances of being admitted, and getting beyond a school's minimum requirements.

- *The Grad School Handbook* — This book discusses the reasons for pursuing a graduate degree, how to find information and make decisions related to it, various ways to finance a graduate school program, submitting an application — including essays and letters of recommendation — and also provides an overview of the standard admissions tests for graduate school. The information provided for returning students and those who are not admitted to graduate school is especially enlightening.

- *Real-Life Guide to Graduate & Professional School* — This publication explains where to start your search for the right graduate school, details the application process, and discusses various aspects of the student's graduate school experience.

- *Kaplan/Newsweek Graduate School Admissions Advisor* — This book contains an introduction to graduate school and examines specific disciplines and the total application process. It also supplies additional information for African-American students, international students, disabled students, and re-entry students who are pursuing a graduate degree.

Tip #68: Part One in the Application Process — Writing Your Admissions Essay

The essay you write will give the admissions committee an

opportunity to get to know you more personally and will distinguish you from other applicants at the same time. With this in mind, you will want to provide a word picture of your distinct personality and underscore that you are highly motivated to obtain your MBA degree at that particular institution. This document can sometimes be the determining factor in regard to your acceptance or rejection by the business school of your choice. Above all, your aim is to write a personal statement that is interesting to the reader, completely honest, and well structured. Here are some steps that should help you in preparing for this:

1. **Learn about the components that make up the admissions essay.** Three key elements of an application essay are its content, its delivery, and correct use of spelling and grammar, and they should blend together well for an overall positive effect. Your first sentence should explain your reasons for wanting to earn an MBA and discuss how you became interested in pursuing a career in management. The body of your essay should deal with topics such as your experiences, your past accomplishments, and any other details that support the points made in your introduction, along with future goals.

Your essay should also contain about three paragraphs, which will flow smoothly if you use transitions and resolutions as you write. The transitional device that begins each paragraph should include a topic sentence, indicating that paragraph's theme, and the concluding sentence should likewise contain a resolution that provides a smooth transition to the next paragraph.

2. **Focus on the most important part of your essay.** This is the subject matter itself, and you should be prepared to spend one to two weeks brainstorming to determine your chosen topic, which is intended to be a clear indicator of your personality.

As you go through the self-study process before you begin writing and learn what your priorities are at that point, remember to take the following steps:

- Consider what you feel are your major accomplishments in the "real world" thus far, outside of the academic environment. Besides your work experience, they may include community or extracurricular activities, which can always be viewed as indicators of your professional potential and leadership capability. While you may have received recognition for some of the things you have done, there may be others that you know were turning points in your life, and they also should be mentioned.

- Try to think of a worthwhile personal trait you have that distinguishes you from others and the way in which you developed it.

- Ask yourself if you were deeply influenced by any elements in our culture, such as books, motion pictures, music, or television, and explain why this is so.

- Think about your most difficult past experience and how it affected the way you view life today.

- While you will be dealing with your successes throughout the application process, you should also consider a significant failure from the past and how you overcame it.

- Ask yourself if you have ever experienced an "A-ha! moment" in which you came to realize that something was important to you for the first time.

- Consider what others would say about you and how they would describe you if they were writing an essay about you.

- Think about your plans for the future and how attending graduate school and earning your MBA fit into the mosaic of your life.

- Be sure to include some vivid personal experiences in your essay, with supporting details. Do not include any information that can be found elsewhere in your application, including the scores from your GRE and GMAT exams.

- Do not choose a topic for your essay that is too broad in scope and would be better suited as the subject of a research paper or a special report. Remember that you want to capture the reader's interest from the first word of your essay. You also need to avoid writing on a topic that is controversial, unless you are willing to take a balanced approach, because doing so may leave a negative impression on the reader.

- When you are writing your essay and going for your

admissions interview, you should be completely open and honest to ensure a positive outcome and that you are being evaluated on your written and oral communication skills in both cases.

3. **Discuss the issue you have chosen to write about thoroughly and carefully.** If you are not totally focused on your topic, your writing style and tone will not be enough to carry you through when you are working on your essay. In addition, if you are truly passionate about your topic, you will be able to present it in an interesting light, no matter what that topic may be. You should be prepared to describe your feelings, as well as your actions, regarding past events you mention in your essay.

4. **Try to create word pictures for your reader by using precise but lively prose.** Avoid vague terms and language that is wordy. Also, since the reader does not know you, try to create interesting parallels and provide pertinent examples to get your message across.

5. **Give the introduction to your essay the importance it deserves.** While you want to capture the admissions officer's interest from the start, do not make the mistake of turning the beginning of your essay into a summary of it. When you have completed the project, check the introduction to see if it needs editing or a complete revision. At the start, you want to appeal to the reader's emotions and pique his or her curiosity, and then make sure that the writing flows smoothly throughout the text.

6. **A good conclusion to your essay is essential.** You will not want to summarize at this point either because your essay

should be relatively brief. Try to link the conclusion to your introduction to create a sense of completeness, indicate that the topic you selected has broad implications, and end on a positive note.

7. **Set the essay aside for a few days when your first draft is complete.** Doing this will enable you to look at what you have written with the "fresh eyes" that editors in the publishing field often recommend. As you edit the piece, you may also want to seek the assistance of others in detecting errors, since you may have automatically memorized certain paragraphs if you have reread them numerous times. After that, check to see if you have remembered to do the following from beginning to end:

   - Use active voice whenever you can, which is less cumbersome for the reader than passive voice, and avoid using trite expressions.

   - Try to vary the sentence structure, use smooth transitional devices to avoid choppiness, and determine if each sentence is vital to the total piece rather than extraneous.

   - See to it that every point you want to make is clear to the reader, with an emphasis on presenting a complete picture of your personality in your essay.

Because editing is such a delicate art, you may need to rearrange paragraphs to make your writing more comprehensive, delete anything that falls into the category of "excess baggage," or add new material to support the points you want to make.

Tip #69: Part Two in the Application Process — Compiling Your Graduate School Résumé

You may consider this the most difficult part of the application to complete because you will want to highlight every aspect of your work experience while keeping word economy in mind. As you do this, use concrete words, such as "organized" and "supervised" in describing your accomplishments and, where you can, indicate how you helped improve your employer's bottom line, including profit increases, improved productivity, cost reduction, and time saved. In addition, do not hesitate to mention any increased responsibilities you were given and any promotions you received because of your efforts on behalf of your organization. Here are some points to consider:

1. **What you should include in your application résumé.** When you are putting your résumé together, place greater emphasis on results and productivity, rather than on the activities you engaged in. Admissions officers always look for indications of leadership ability and positive project results when they are accepting applicants to business school.

This is also a good place to highlight your extracurricular or group activities as examples of your leadership ability, your multitasking skills, and your versatility. As you do this, you must be prepared to pinpoint the contribution you made to a particular activity's success, instead of implying that you just "went along for the ride." At the same time, do not reveal information you know is too personal to be relevant on your application, and think before providing details related to your religious or political connections that the reader may consider too controversial. You may want to mention your hobbies and other interests, but only if you feel they fit in with the personal goals you have indicated as part of your application.

2. **Why your application résumé is important.** It is the primary tool you have at your disposal for marketing yourself, and admissions officers expect it to provide a record of your academic and career accomplishments and to indicate how they relate to your desire for graduate study and your plans for the future. You will need to present the information you provide, especially that which relates to your career goals, accurately and completely without adding any personal or editorial comment, much like a good news reporter.

3. **What admissions officers expect from your résumé.** They look for clear-cut evidence that you are prepared to enroll in their graduate program and advance your career, and that your work experience is relevant to them and to your future employers. They also expect complete honesty from you, and you should not hesitate to mention that you were laid off at some point because of a reduction in force, for example, since such a deliberate omission can have unforeseen side effects on your admission to business school.

Losing your job in such a situation is not a reflection on you; instead, it is an indicator of your former employer's financial health or the general state of the economy at the time. If the thought of undergoing a thorough background check is something you would find difficult to live with for some reason, you should either reconsider applying to graduate school or come to terms with the situation. (This topic is discussed in detail in Chapter I.)

Tip #70: Part Three in the Application Process — Submitting Your Letters of Recommendation

You will be asked to submit three of letters of recommendation as part of your application, including at least one from an individual who has supervised you closely and is prepared to discuss your work performance in detail, rather than your academic achievements in undergraduate school. This type of recommendation will also carry more weight than a letter from someone who has mere "name recognition" in the admissions office, such as a politician, an entertainer, or a former student. The following points are essential:

1. **Why these letters are required for admission to graduate school.** Admissions officers use letters of recommendation as a means of verifying or detailing your academic history, your work experience, your abilities, and your goals. They also regard them as a tool to be used in forming an overall opinion of you as a candidate for their MBA program. When you receive the recommendation forms from the business school of your choice, you will have to determine if you want to waive or retain your right to see those recommendations after they are submitted. You may find that professors who have taught you in the past refuse to submit such a letter unless it is kept confidential. Also, admissions officers tend to give more importance to recommendations they receive that fall into the confidential category.

2. **What type of recommendation the admissions officers expect you to submit.** Business schools require a specific number of these letters, and you should not exceed that number, since your aim is to complete your application exactly as directed. Also, administrators are interested in the quality of your recommendations, rather than the quantity of the letters you submit. Your complete application will be viewed as a single, integrated unit, and there should be a definite correlation between the strengths indicated in your letters of recommendation and those mentioned elsewhere in your application materials.

Tip #71: How to Simplify Things for Those Who Write Letters for You

Since you will be asking your "recommenders" for a favor, you will want to make the process of writing a letter for you as uncomplicated and pleasant as possible. You can accomplish this by providing them with an overall picture of yourself as a potential graduate student in a packet of pertinent material. Taking such a step will show them that you are a well-organized, serious student who deserves their recommendation.

1. **What your recommendation packet should include.** As you put your packet together, be sure that it contains the following items:

    - A copy of your completed admissions résumé, which is your business school "marketing tool."

- A copy of your undergraduate transcript. If it contains anything that can be viewed in an unfavorable light, such as dropping out one semester due to a family emergency, include a brief, unemotional note of explanation.

- Pertinent information about every business school to which you are applying, with each one listed individually. Discuss that school's MBA program; explain how it dovetails with your interests and goals, using some of the information you have gathered from your research; and limit each listing to about two sentences.

You also will want to refer to your statement of purpose when you complete this part of the packet.

2. **Why you will need to send a cover letter with your packet.** The cover letter you include with the packet will eliminate confusion over deadlines, and the people you approach for a recommendation will feel much more at ease. The material you have compiled will also prove helpful in other ways as you go through the admissions process.

3. **Emphasizing your work experience in your application.** This is a significant factor in admitting applicants to any MBA program, because a student who has some experience in the working world can better relate to concepts presented to them in their graduate courses, which emphasize group activity and student participation in class. Full-time work experience matters most in this case, as opposed to any summer internships and part-time jobs listed on your résumé.

4. **Emphasizing your leadership skills in your application.** Think of times when you led an organization or spearheaded a project, even if you were never named as the official leader of the staff or team under discussion. Also, try thinking about the skills that an individual needs to manage a business well, and then provide examples to show how you have developed those skills and that you want to make further progress by acquiring your MBA.

Tip #72: Part Three — Being Proactive with Your Graduate School Interview

Since admission to graduate school has become increasingly competitive, interviews with applicants have also become increasingly common on many college campuses. Both faculty members and potential students have a stake in them because they will be interacting with one another for a relatively long time if the applicant is accepted into the program. If an admissions interview is part of your chosen business school's application process, it may also prove to be the most important one. Taking the initiative by requesting an interview, if it is optional in your situation, is something you will want to consider.

1. **When a by-invitation-only interview is part of your application.** The business schools that use this type of interview are quite selective, and they often have a large database of applicants waiting to be admitted into their program. Such interviews are scheduled to clarify material contained in the candidate's application, including the essay or résumé, and if you are asked to participate in one, be sure to handle any questions the interviewer may have for you as skillfully and sincerely as you can.

From the administration's perspective, the admissions interview can be used as one of its marketing tools, and the interviewer is likely to highlight the best features of the school's MBA program when you meet. You will also have an opportunity to build rapport with that person, demonstrate what you have to offer the school, and indicate your interest in their business program. Show how your work experience and undergraduate training have prepared you for earning your MBA.

2. **When a mandatory interview is part of your application.** When an interview is required to complete the application process, the administration is aiming to assess your individual strengths and determine whether you will function well in the school's unique cultural and academic environment. Knowing this, you will find it easier to remain calm during the interview if you keep the following factors in mind:

- **What you can expect at your admissions interview.** There are many types of admissions interviews, including the one-on-one, group, and telephone categories, and they are all important in the application process. You can prepare for your interview by researching the MBA program the school has to offer and the departmental faculty. Be ready to discuss your individual career goals, and talk about how having an advanced degree will help you reach them. In addition, during the interview, you should try to bring certain aspects of your admissions essay to life, which will allow your personality to shine, and your communication skills will be evaluated accordingly.

- **What you should do at your admissions interview.** Dress professionally, as you would if you were applying for a job, and be prompt in keeping your appointment. In the course of the interview, make it clear that you intend to focus on your graduate work and want to advance your career in management. This is also an opportune time to ask questions about the school's MBA program and those involved in it, as an indication that you are interested and have familiarized yourself with what the school has to offer its business students.

Answer the interviewer's questions with honesty and candor, because this individual is an expert at interpreting body language, which should never belie what you are saying. In other words, this is not the time for you to test your acting ability.

- **What you need to remember about admissions interviews.** Whether you have a formal interview as part of your school's admission process, contact you have with anyone connected to the business school — students, alumni, faculty, or staff — is important. Regardless of the circumstances, it is always possible for you to make an impression, both positive and negative, on someone who will play a role in determining the fate of your application.

Tip #73: Using an Admissions Consultant in Your Search for the Right Business School

If you feel your background is a bit unusual in some aspects when compared with the backgrounds of others who enroll in business school and that you may have difficulty in gaining admission as a result, this is an option you may want to consider, despite the additional cost. If you take this step, you will be given an independent, expert opinion by someone who will study your application from the viewpoint of an admissions officer.

The admissions consultant you choose, who may even be a former admissions officer, will often have special knowledge related to the individual schools you are considering and can provide valuable information that will help you in making your decision. Consider taking this step to level the playing field, since many other applicants who plan to acquire an MBA will be using admissions consultants successfully.

Tip #74: What You Should Do When a Business School Accepts Your Application

If you are accepted into a graduate program, be sure to respond by the indicated deadline or the school may rescind the offer. Do not assume you will be able to transfer any credits you accumulate while enrolled in the business school if you decide to transfer out of that school's program. If you are fortunate enough to be offered admission by several business schools, fine-tune the elements of your search and zero in on the program that seems to be the best "fit" for you.

Although it may be possible for you to defer your enrollment once you are accepted, try to avoid doing so unless unforeseen illness, a family crisis, or an unexpected assignment at work with new responsibilities makes taking this step an absolute necessity.

Tip #75: What Your Response to the Business School Should Be

When you are notified of your acceptance into a graduate program, the admissions committee will appreciate your promptness and honesty in responding, since your decision may affect the fate of other candidates. Some business schools may try to pressure you into making a decision regarding your enrollment before April 15, which is inappropriate, since you do not have to decide until that date. At the same time, if you do accept an offer of admission, you are committed to that acceptance, and you should avoid attempting to be released from it, unless it is absolutely necessary, because of the unpleasant academic "fallout" that may result.

Whenever you accept or decline an admission, send the school a brief e-mail, call, or fax a letter addressed to your contact person, or to the entire admissions committee, thanking them for their offer and telling them about your decision. Then send a follow-up letter in the regular mail to avoid any confusion or misunderstanding regarding your plans by providing an original hard copy for their files.

Conclusion

Applying to a graduate school for admission into their MBA program can be a complicated, time-consuming process made up of many factors. They include your undergraduate scholastic record, your GRE and GMAT test scores, your admissions essay, your admissions résumé, your letters of recommendation, and your admissions interview.

Chapter 8
Consider Getting an MBA Degree Online

In this type of program, known as "distance learning," instructors and their students do not meet face to face. Education is mainly accomplished through interactive classes on the Internet. Here, the use of audio communication is considered an essential component in maintaining contact between students and their instructors, along with various modern teaching strategies based on the latest computer applications.

Tip #76: Some Distance-Learning Possibilities That May Suit Your Needs

Whether you plan to study part-time or full-time to earn your MBA, attending classes through the Internet may be the option that seems most viable in your particular circumstances. It may be especially appealing to you if you often travel on business or relocate frequently for your current employer. Your graduate studies will always be "portable" if you study online, and you will not have to concern yourself with transferring credits if you move to a new location. Here are some factors to consider:

1. **What your distance-learning courses will be like.** If you

decide to go the distance-learning route, you will not be hindered by strict schedules or limited program choices available on campuses in your geographic area. As a rule, exercising the distance-learning option will enable you to log on for "class" at a time that is convenient for you and participate in discussion and debates in a forum that somewhat resembles an Internet "chat room."

Depending on the distance-learning program you choose, you may participate in synchronous (live) classes or asynchronous (non-live) classes. You will also interact with your fellow students and your professors by using "virtual classrooms. "Virtual group projects are another possibility. You must be prepared to work with your fellow students as part of a team, just as you would if you were taking classes on campus. You will either complete your assignments, tests, and quizzes online or use a designated software program, and then submit them to your instructor by e-mail to be graded.

2. **Discovering more about your distance-learning program.** The typical online business school offers demonstrations on their Web site, which will allow you to preview this type of educational experience before you commit yourself to it. An orientation class may be included and, at that time, you will meet the instructors, staff, and other students; be given the technical information you will need to proceed; and find out how to get started with your classes. You will also learn about the technology used in the course, the available tools needed to begin the program, and resources that are available to you, such as the business school's library facilities.

3. **The amount of time you will be investing in your courses.**

The amount of time it will take to earn your online MBA degree will vary, depending on the business school and the area of specialization you choose. For example, you can complete an intensive MBA program in nine months or study online for up to four years. Also, some institutions are flexible in accommodating the individual student's needs and circumstances, while others find it necessary to impose more stringent deadlines on those who participate in their program in an effort to uphold their academic standards.

4. **The standard MBA curriculum for distance learning.** An online business school program includes participating in classes, required reading, and online interaction with instructors and students. It may also provide multimedia elements, like podcasting, video conferencing, and video lectures. In addition, you may be expected to be present for some workshops or courses as you accumulate the "residency hours" required by the program. In some cases, all mandatory testing is done in the student's local area.

Tip #77: How You Can Tell if You Are Prepared to Study Online

Regardless of their age, background, or work experience, all online students need to possess the following characteristics to benefit from their classes and complete their graduate program successfully:

- **Being ready to share your life, work, and educational past as part of the ongoing learning process.** If you are an introvert, doing this should be less difficult for you than it would be if you were attending class on campus, because distance learning will eliminate the visual barriers that can sometimes hinder a shy student's self-expression in a traditional classroom.

- **Acknowledging that decision making and critical thinking are essential to the program.** These are two characteristics that a manager sorely needs, and as a student, you will make decisions based on information you are given and your life experience to prepare for a managerial role. This activity involves the use of critical thought, which you will exercise in the case-study process, and it will be an essential part of your online program.

- **Being prepared to communicate with others through your writing.** If you feel deficient in this area, take some prep courses before you enroll in a program such as this, where good writing skills are a prerequisite for admission.

- **Being ready to let your instructor know if you are having a problem with the course material.** Teachers on every level look for nonverbal cues from their students, including body language, to determine if anyone in the class is having some kind of difficulty, and they try to provide the help the student needs. However, since it will not be possible for your instructor to do this if you study online, you will have to take the initiative if you feel you need some assistance and contact your instructor.

- **Being prepared to set aside four to fifteen hours weekly for each course you take.** You will have to invest time and money if you want to succeed in obtaining your online MBA and benefit from the program. You should expect to participate in your online classroom from five to seven days every week.

- **Being able to consider ideas carefully before giving your response.** This enables you to provide significant input into your virtual classroom participation as various concepts are tested and challenged, just as they are in the business world and college classrooms every day. If you are a nontraditional student who has difficulty in dealing with traditional teaching methods and class lectures, or if you are hindered in enrolling for your MBA by your schedule limitations, prohibitive tuition costs, or other constraints, this may be exactly the type of program you need.

- **Being able to balance your family obligations and your graduate program.** Since you will be doing your course work at home, you will need the support and cooperation of every family member if you are going to succeed. Explain to them that your schedule outside of work is going to change because you will soon have "school work" to do.

Tip #78: Factors Involved in Distance Learning for You to Consider

You will also want to keep the following in mind:

1. **Benefits of distance-learning MBA programs.** For many

people, this method of studying is convenient because they are not obliged to follow a traditional semester schedule to earn the credits they need. Also, since it can be adjusted to your particular circumstances, you, as a student, will set the pace of your graduate program. Studying this way can be less expensive than studying the traditional way and, of course, arranging for housing will not be a concern for you.

Once you have reviewed the pluses and minuses of distance education, you can examine online graduate programs that appeal to you and determine if they are compatible with your individual needs and obligations. Also, while certain programs may have an in-class component at some point, you will still save travel time and the expense that getting to every class on campus entails.

2. **Negative factors involved in distance-learning MBA programs.** If you take this approach to completing a graduate program, your interaction with your professors and classmates will be limited to discussion groups, chat rooms, and e-mail, and you will have to be self-motivated and not at all inclined to procrastinate. You will also need to use your own resources for completing various projects and preparing for tests. In addition, the unique culture of the graduate school you choose will be unfamiliar to you, since you will be studying away from campus.

3. **Keeping your employer's viewpoint on distance learning in mind.** While your current employer or a prospective employer may be skeptical about your online MBA, they are far more likely to acknowledge its validity if your degree comes from an accredited, well-established

business school. This is especially true of online businesses; technology companies; and the marketing, media, and communications industries. Overall acceptance of distance learning is growing in the general job market today.

Tip #79: What You Can Do to Reassure Your Employer About Your Online MBA

If you feel you need to be proactive in clearing up any misunderstanding that may exist in the business world regarding your distance-learning training, you can always include the following information on your résumé or in a job interview as a preventive measure:

- You have developed your technological skills and gained business experience while you completed your graduate program.

- Earning your degree online has helped you become self-motivated, practice self-discipline, and become skilled in the art of time management, because the schedule you followed was more flexible and self-determined than it would have been in a traditional classroom setting.

- Good communication skills were essential in completing your online course of study, because you participated in networking and interacted with your fellow students and instructors via the Internet.

- You are prepared to provide samples of your class assignments and projects that hold up well when compared to activities that took place on your school's campus simultaneously. In addition, you may want to include your graduate school transcripts, letters of recommendation from your instructors, and proof of the institution's accreditation when you are job hunting.

Tip #80: Ways of Paying for Your Online Education

If your graduate school has what is known as "Title IV status," you should have the same financial aid options as students who attend class on campus, but you may have some difficulty in applying for it. You can find out if scholarships are available for distance-learning students, and you may qualify for certain federal student loans, as indicated below:

- **Stafford Loans.** These loans are available to undergraduate and graduate students in varying amounts, based on their particular circumstances and criteria the applicant must meet to obtain them. With the usual unsubsidized Stafford Loan, you will be responsible for paying the interest once the six-month grace period after you receive your MBA comes to an end. These loans are guaranteed to have a low interest rate in line with your budget, and their main purpose is to help students realize their goal of obtaining their degree.

As another option, you may want to work with the government-designated agency in the state where you will be studying to obtain a Stafford Loan that will be funded by tax-exempt bonds, or you can work with private institutions like Bank of

America, Sun Trust, or Wachovia. Such a loan may include an additional incentive if you agree to direct-withdrawal loan payments from your bank account or make regular on-time payments yourself.

- **Perkins Loans.** If you qualify for one of these loans, you will receive low interest rates, favorable long-term payment choices, and larger sums of money. These loans must be reapplied for annually, have a maximum of $40,000 at the graduate level, and come with a 90-day grace period for the borrower. Your loan will be disbursed directly through the business school you attend, and you can consult your financial aid adviser about extending the payment terms or requesting a loan deferment if the need arises.

- **The Career Training Loan.** This type of loan is offered by Sallie Mae, a private lending source, and it covers the entire cost of tuition and additional expenses. To qualify, you must be a U.S. citizen or an eligible non-citizen and be enrolled on a part-time basis. If necessary, you can apply with a co-signer, a $1,000 minimum loan is required, and the interest rate you are charged for the loan will be based on your credit rating. For more information, or to complete your loan application, visit Sallie Mae's Web site at **http:// salliemae.com or call 1-888-272-5543.**

- **The Access Group.** This is another private loan source intended for individuals who are enrolled in a graduate program. Loans are available to students who want to complete their course of study at their own pace, which allows for greater flexibility. Those who apply for such a loan may receive up to the full cost of their tuition, and the loan may also be administered by the business school itself. In that case, you can contact your online institution to find out what loans are available to you.

Conclusion

Taking graduate courses online is a viable alternative to traditional studying on campus, which may interest you because of this method's flexibility. Here are some points to consider before you choose this option:

- Whether you are sufficiently motivated to study online and what you will need to do to complete the program.

- How you will finance your courses in this situation.

- Reassuring your employer or a potential employer in regard to distance learning.

Chapter 9
The Demands of the Graduate School Curriculum

As an undergraduate student, you were provided with basic information on a wide range of topics without delving into any one of those topics deeply. In business school, the skills you need to succeed and the goals that are established will be quite different. Once you are aware of the change, become convinced of its importance, and are determined to adjust to it, you will be able to get the most out of your graduate school experience.

Why So Many Things Are Different in a Graduate Program

As you begin your studies, you will find there is a shift in emphasis from simply memorizing essential information to comprehending and analyzing it more fully, which will be aided by the research you do as part of the program, along with an intensive amount of reading that is always part of the curriculum. You will also be tested much less frequently in business school, because it will be less important for you to recall a particular fact and more important for you to know where information can be found. This means you will be able to approach the subject matter presented to you from your unique perspective and see how it fits in with your educational and career goals.

The Types of Assignments You Will Be Given in Business School

When you work on a written assignment as part of your program, your task will be to highlight clear, well-supported arguments and critique and make use of information you have gathered. Do not be intimidated by the lengthy list of recommended reading your professors may provide. Some of the items on that list will be supplemental material you can refer to in order to gain greater insight into the subject matter or the purpose of the course you are taking, but you will not be expected to read all of them.

Tip #81: Having the Right Outlook Toward Graduate School

At this point in your life, you will be filling many roles, and you may find you are looked on as a business professional, a classmate, a team member, and a researcher simultaneously. Along with that, you will be treated as a colleague and a student by your instructors as you are completing your coursework and earning your degree, especially if you are a graduate school assistant or completing an internship. While this may be perplexing, it is also quite normal, and if you try to remain calm, you will adjust to the situation in time.

You may also find that taking the following steps is as essential to your success as completing your class assignments:

1. **Realize that doing research may be an important part of your MBA program.** At the start of the semester, decide which professors you would like to work with and make an appointment with them to discuss research topics they are working on. If any of those topics interest you, offer your help in completing the project, learn to write your own grant proposals related to it, and consult with other people who have done similar work to benefit from their experience.

2. **Learn to network to get the most out of your program and advance your career.** As you go through your course of study, make it a point to do some networking, to stay up to date with the latest business trends, and to become a known entity. As your schedule permits, read related journals to stay current on the latest research trends, join professional organizations, attend pertinent workshops and conferences, and be prepared to take part in presentations at business meetings and other events.

3. **Maintain balance in your life by having at least one outside interest while you study.** In the beginning, you may feel you have to treat graduate school as one long marathon race, but you will never reach the finish line if you take that approach. Instead, find or continue to participate in some activity that is unrelated to the intense concentration, stress, and competition you encounter in business school and on the job. Such an outside interest can be as varied as biking or gardening, and the choice is yours.

4. **Keep track of your various academic deadlines to avoid confusion and stress.** List all appointments, test dates, and report deadlines on your monthly calendar to avoid being

taken by surprise when the day arrives. You can also include self-imposed due dates for completing long-term projects, which should be broken down into their component parts to make them more manageable. Taking this approach will help you in learning to "think like a manager," which is something you should be anxious to do. In addition, some items, such as meeting with your study group or attending a class, will be taking place every week with few exceptions, and your calendar can be supplemented with a daily to-do list to help you stay on track.

5. **Make it a point to do some "school work" every day.** It is better to allot some time to working on class assignments or research on a daily basis, instead of planning one or two marathon sessions on the weekend. By doing this, you will find the subject matter seems more familiar to you, and you will also have to spend less time in reviewing old material. As an added bonus, you will be able to take unexpected, unavoidable interruptions of your study time in stride because this approach will help you become more flexible and will reduce your stress level.

6. **Realize that the stress in our lives can be a two-edged sword.** Most of us would agree that a certain amount of "healthy tension" or stress in our lives keeps us motivated, helps us to prepare for and adapt to change, and enables us to face challenges as they come along. At the same time, we need to take control of it to keep stress from degenerating into anxiety and damaging our health, our relationships, and our careers. If we feel stress on the job or in an academic setting, it can be a sign that the activities related to what are expected to do and our capabilities and inclinations are not well matched.

7. **Learn what you can do to improve the situation.** Here are some steps you can take to keep the stress you feel under control:

   - Learn to eat a healthy diet, and limit your intake of caffeine and refined sugar, which can cause frequent changes in your blood glucose levels. You should also determine the amount of sleep you need every night to be productive and learn to set realistic goals for yourself. Many people have adopted a relaxation technique — yoga, mediation, or prayer — to reduce the amount of stress in their daily lives, along with developing a good sense of humor and a positive outlook.

   - Try to be forgiving of yourself and others: "Yesterday is history, tomorrow is a mystery, and today is a gift." In other words, waste no time on the past, except to learn from your mistakes; plan for the future as best you can; and learn to live in the present. Be ready to take initiative when the occasion calls for it, but treat people with respect as well.

8. **Coping with stress can affect your mental and physical well-being.** Short-term stress (taking the GMAT) and long-term stress (getting through a graduate program) can affect you physically, and these effects can become acute or chronic. Poor concentration, difficulty sleeping, digestive problems, depression, and headaches are all indications that we may be overly stressed. If you reach the point where you are dealing with your stress by abusing tobacco, alcohol, or other drugs, or often become angry, seeking professional help should be your only option.

9. **Try to establish good rapport with your instructors.** We know that first impressions are important, and if a professor begins by thinking you are an interested, responsible student, this concept will carry over when your coursework is evaluated. As a result, that professor's expectation will be that the class assignments you submit will meet the business school's professional standards. Conversely, if you manage to create the impression that you have an indifferent or hostile attitude toward your studies, that will have the opposite effect. This sorry phenomenon is sometimes referred to as a "self-fulfilling prophecy."

10. **Get help from your instructor when you feel you need it.** At some point during your graduate studies, the time will come when you have to consult with one of your professors to complete a particular course successfully. It is much better to take this step when you find you have run into a problem than to wait until the situation has become critical or embarrassingly obvious.

Common reasons for needing such assistance include the following:

- You have missed class because of illness or need help understanding the subject matter.

- You need clarification about the requirements related to a particular project or assignment, certain school policies, or related scheduling requirements.

Students sometimes avoid taking this step because of their shyness or because they fear such a meeting may turn out to be confrontational. They may also feel their questions will seem foolish, or they may tend to avoid interacting with any authority figure unless it is absolutely necessary. To resolve the problem you are facing and get the help you need, you will have to overcome any anxiety you may feel and show the maturity it takes to acknowledge your limitations and the respect you have for your instructor.

11. **Learn the right way to ask for help.** If you know how to go about doing this and take the following steps, you will be more at ease when you decide to consult with your instructor:

- Begin by finding out your professor's preferred mode of contact and regular office hours. If the need is not urgent, you may want to try e-mail and then wait a few days for a reply that answers your questions, or suggest a time when the two of you could meet. When you make your request for an appointment, indicate that you want to choose a time that is convenient for your instructor.

- Once your meeting is scheduled, prepare a list of questions to ask your instructor that will enable you to accomplish what you need to in one session. You should also be prepared to take notes when you meet. Be on time for your appointment, and thank your professor for providing his or her assistance as you leave.

What Your Course Load Will Be Like in Business School

Once you enroll for classes, you can expect weekly assignments in your economics and accounting courses, and you will learn to give presentations in your marketing and management classes. In addition, to balance critical theory with a problem-solving approach, most MBA programs include team projects and case studies as essential components of their core curriculum.

Working with Case Studies as Part of Your MBA Program

Case studies are detailed accounts of an industry, company, project, or person over a specified time. The information considered part of a case study may include data related to the subject's strategies, goals, challenges, recommendations, and other related factors. In addition, a case study may be brief or quite detailed, and it can vary in length, from a two-page summary to a complex report of over thirty pages.

Case studies will be part of your MBA program, because they are intended to teach students how to analyze a business situation and then make an appropriate decision based on the analysis, which is what will be expected of them when they assume the role of manager. Since this is the policy, during a typical two-year MBA program, you may work with as many as 800 of these case studies by the time you complete the program.

Other Factors That Will Be Part of Your Graduate School Experience

1. **Your MBA core curriculum courses in detail.** The courses in this category form the basis of any MBA curriculum, and

they will be taken in the earlier part of your program. They include accounting, finance, economics, marketing, human resources, manufacturing, statistics, operations, business strategy, and technology. Enrollment in these basic courses is often quite high, and you will want to know if you will be assigned to smaller work groups and have satisfactory access to the faculty. This will enable you to master the material presented in class more easily.

2. **What your graduate courses will emphasize.** The typical business school core curriculum focuses on the following areas:

   - Your accounting courses will provide you with an overview of accounting, including the terminology and concepts you need to function effectively in the business and financial worlds, and their proper application is essential for anyone who assumes a managerial role and works with budgets.

   - In your marketing and economics courses, you will discover that these fields also have their own unique terminology, which you will learn to master.

   - Two courses that may be part of your MBA program are intended to provide you with the business tools you need as a manager. The first one will include the practical tools you will use to comprehend, analyze, and solve the problems you will face in the financial and statistical areas of business. The second one will focus on various simulation and quantitative methods, presenting opportunities for you to deal with various computer-based situations you will encounter in the "real-world" atmosphere of today's competitive business environment.

3. **Additional MBA courses you may take.** Other core courses that are part of a business school's management training program include:

   - **Business Ethics**, in which moral values are analyzed and applied to the day-to-day conduct of business.

   - **Human and Organizational Behavior**, which provides psychological insight regarding human behavior and studies people's reactions in specific situations.

   - **Marketing Strategy and Development**, which will help you master basic marketing concepts and improve your creative thinking and problem-solving skills.

   - **Operations Strategy and Business Strategy**, two closely related courses that are part of a business school's core curriculum for their MBA program.

4. **Your MBA elective courses in detail.** The courses in this category will enable you to concentrate on your chosen field of study to complement your management courses and develop your expertise in that area. If you are going to be a part-time student, determine what electives will be available to you on that basis and find out what the school's policy is in regard to canceling such courses so that you will not be taken by surprise. You should also know when you need to declare your area of concentration and

if double-majors are permitted. You may be able to take elective courses apart from the business school within the larger institution and still earn credits toward your MBA, but you will need to clarify that when you enroll to avoid any misunderstanding later.

5. **What you should ask when you are ready to register for your graduate classes.** You should know if this is done by open enrollment, a lottery, or something similar; when the course schedule will be available; how schedule changes are handled; what is considered a typical course load; and if you will be assigned to an academic advisor. You want a faculty member for your advisor who is well respected, has research interests that are similar to your own, and can provide the guidance you will need as you complete the course of study.

6. **Why a having good academic advisor can make a real difference.** Most schools establish a general code of ethics and a definite quota on how many students an advisor can monitor. Unfortunately, acting as an advisor to students is often not a high priority for business school professors because of other realities in their professional lives. Often, they receive little or no recognition for assuming this role; it has no bearing on their salary increases, personal prestige, or consideration for promotion; and they tend to focus more on their research.

While you have the main responsibility for managing your graduate studies and the success of your career, your academic advisor can also play a key role here. Along with guiding you through the curriculum, this individual can write letters of recommendation for you or assist you in finding a management position once you have earned your MBA. As a student, remember that your advisor's time is limited, and this individual will want you to provide updates on the progress you are making. Ask for advice when you need it, and make a genuine effort to maintain a good relationship with him or her. You may also decide to join a study group or select a tutor from the list provided by your school.

Conclusion

Adjusting to the demands of graduate school will not be easy, especially if you are taking courses while holding down a full-time job. In addition, you will find that your business school experience is far different from your undergraduate days. Here are some things to remember as your courses begin:

- Having the right attitude about earning your MBA is essential.

- You must be prepared to complete case studies and conduct research.

- You should have an overview of the entire course of study.

- You will be working with an academic advisor.

CHAPTER 10
HOW THE GRE WILL FIT INTO YOUR PLAN

The GRE (Graduate Record Exam) is a computer-adaptive test (CAT) that you will need to take before you apply to business school. It is offered frequently from October through June each year. This exam is given at designated testing centers using private computer stations, and paper-based test centers are used in parts of the world where the CAT format is unavailable.

Why the GRE Is Required as Part of the MBA Admissions Process

Many colleges and universities consider this test an indicator of the applicant's future success in earning an advanced degree. It is looked on as a useful evaluation tool because potential students come from an array of undergraduate schools, and the standards at these institutions vary. Since the GRE is a general test, it is not directly related to any individual field of study, and admissions officers will also use the GMAT, the subject test for students applying to business school, to measure how well you will fit into their graduate business program.

Tip #82: What Taking the GRE Exam Is Like

The total completion time for the test is about three hours, and the directions provided for each section indicate the total number of items contained in that section and the amount of time given to complete it. You will also find that each section presents its own unique challenges, as it assesses your skill in several areas. The exam is made up of the following components:

1. **The verbal reasoning section.** In this section, the applicant is expected to analyze written material comprehensively, including the parts of sentences and the relationship between a concept and a word that represents the idea. Thirty minutes are allotted for this part of the exam.

2. **The quantitative reasoning section.** This section will test your basic mathematical skills and your ability to solve problems. In answering these questions, you will also be dealing with quantitative comparisons and data interpretation. Forty-five minutes are allotted for the completion of twenty-eight questions.

3. **The analytical writing section.** This section is made up of two parts, the issues portion and the argument portion, and both serve the purpose of testing your skill in expressing complex concepts clearly and effectively, examining statements and the evidence they contain, and supporting your conclusions with appropriate specifics in an understandable, coherent manner.

- **Part I.** The issues portion tests the student's grasp of basic concepts of data analysis, geometry, algebra, arithmetic, and the ability to solve problems on an advanced level, and 45 minutes are allotted to complete it. You will be provided with a choice of two subjects of general interest, and you will be free to state your personal opinion on the topic you choose.

4. **Taking the right approach in answering Part I.** At this point, you will have a certain amount of leeway as you respond to each issue presented. Remember the following points when you formulate your answer:

   - Decide whether you agree with the statement in whole or in part, and consider your reasons for doing so.

   - Determine if the statement is always valid or only valid under certain circumstances and whether you need to define some of the terms being used.

   - See if you can back up the stand you take on the issue under consideration by supplying concrete examples to support your view, determine what counterclaims can be made, and decide how you would handle them.

- **Part II.** The argument portion will require you to read and dissect the case being presented and proceed from there. By way of contrast with Part I, here, you will be required to determine if the argument presented to you is based on sound logic instead of explaining why you agree or disagree with it.

5. **Taking the right approach in answering Part II.** To prepare for this section before test day, try working on several practice items, sticking to the 30-minute time limit and using the following steps:

- Look for the basis of the argument and its conclusion, and see if you can think of any alternative explanations that could be presented.

- Ask yourself what additional evidence would add to or detract from the validity of the argument.

How You Can Register for the GRE Test

The easiest way to do this is by going online to **http://www.gre.org,** an ETS Web site, and filling out an application. You can also register by calling 1-800-GRE-CALL (1-800-473-2255). Test centers tend to fill up quickly, and it is recommended that you register early and take the test as soon as you can, thereby ensuring your scores will be received at the graduate school of your choice in a timely manner.

When you register for the exam, you will be asked to indicate your preferred test center and date, which will be confirmed when your registration is processed. You will receive your admission ticket for the test about three weeks later.

When You Should Register for the GRE Test

While late registration is also online for an additional $25 fee, early registration is often the key to obtaining a scholarship, teaching assistantship, or much-needed financial aid for your MBA program because of the time constraints related to securing them.

Tip #83: Using the GRE Search Service to Find the Right Business School

This service, which will be available to you when you register for the GRE®, coordinates applicants with fellowship sponsors and participating institutions of higher learning that have recruitment profiles in place in a database. If you match one of these profiles, you can receive information related to the admission standards, the programs being offered at that graduate school, the school's financial aid program, and other relevant topics. These may include graduate fellowships, teaching assistant openings, work-study programs, and scholarships.

If you choose to participate in this program, your contact and background information will be sent to the service's database, enabling you to be contacted as a candidate for admission to business school. Your personal information, your educational background, and your educational objectives, including your chosen area of concentration, preference for full- or part-time study, geographic area, and the date you plan to enroll for graduate work are also included.

Tip #84: How to Prepare for the GRE Test

To feel secure in facing the challenge on test day, the wise student will become acquainted with the GRE format, and there are many ways of preparing for it. Pertinent information can be found in a variety of sources, ranging from the official test bulletin to taking a course on GRE preparation. While most prep courses include informative guide books, practice tests, and the use of appropriate software, experts in the field indicate that it is best not to rely on only one source of information when you are preparing to take this test.

You will also find that the official GRE bulletins explain the requirements for taking the exam, along with relevant publications you can buy and a valid test registration form. Visit the Web sites of established testing services for more information, including related programs you may decide to download or purchase. You should use software that is user-friendly for the best results, whether you choose a program that is available in a testing or tutorial mode.

1. **Some publications you can use in your preparation for the GRE.** Some books that may be helpful when you are getting ready to take the GRE exam include:

    - *GRE: Practicing to Take the General Test.* This guide, which is published by Educational Testing Service, contains basic information on preparing for the exam, practice questions, and complete practice tests that were previously administered to GRE applicants.

    - *Kaplan GRE, GMAT Math Exams Workbook.* This is a detailed review of the material contained in the math sections of the GRE and GMAT exams, and it also contains test-taking strategies and various tips intended to maximize your score.

    - *GRE Prep Coures.* This book includes a complete math

review, provides information related to the logic section, helps the student understand the reading comprehension questions contained in the test, lists the 4,000 most commonly used words found in the GRE, and comes with test-preparation software.

- *The Ultimate Math Refresher for the GRE, GMAT, and SAT.* This workbook reviews basic rules and principles of arithmetic, algebra, and geometry for all three exams mentioned in the title. It also provides a variety of practice items in those areas.

- *GRE: Practicing to Take the General Test.* This guide, published by ETS, contains practice test questions along with full-length practice tests that were formerly administered to business school applicants.

2. **Taking practice tests to get ready for the GRE exam.** The use of practice tests may be the most helpful preparation method of all, and the best tests explain the reason behind the correct answer. Prep courses for the GRE may produce impressive results, but they are also expensive. They vary in scope, and the companies that offer them often provide individual tutoring or small classes for those who need them as part of their program.

3. **Using the special software that is available to you as you prepare for the test.** The GRE *Powerprep*® software may be downloaded from the official GRE Web site. It is also mailed to anyone who registers for the CAT version of the test. It contains two sample GRE exams for the verbal and quantitative sections, pertinent analytic writing subjects

and essays, and recommended strategies to use when taking the test.

Powerprep also includes a computer tutorial that allows you to become familiar with the functions of the computer you will be using at the test center, such as the scroll bar and the mouse. Using this software, you can download the math review or try to answer the interactive sample questions it contains.

Other free, official preparation materials for the GRE exam are available at **http://www.ets.org**, and other useful items may be purchased for a small fee at this site.

4. **Testing accommodations for those who have a disability.** The Americans with Disabilities Act (ADA) states accommodations made for a student with a documented disability must be reasonable and individualized, since no type of adjustment may be sufficient or appropriate for everyone who has a particular disability. You may be able to take the GRE test under standard conditions if a minor adjustment at the test site is all that is required, such as providing a sign-language interpreter to translate spoken directions, wheelchair access, or a large-print test book with no extended time for completing any section of the exam. As a rule, your GRE score report will not indicate the test was taken with any accommodations.

Tip #85: How to Deal with the Computerized GRE Exam

Since the test you will be taking is paperless, the following points will help as you prepare to answer the questions on test day:

- The GRE is administered with a special, basic word processor designed by ETS to ensure that those in the group who are familiar with more complex computer programs and know how to use them, do not have an unfair advantage over anyone taking the test who is not so computer-savvy. In other words, a level playing field is provided for everyone, and the software will permit you to perform various actions easily, including inserting text, undoing the previous action, moving and deleting text, and scrolling.

- As you go through the test, be sure to answer each question in the order indicated, because the computer system will choose the next question for you based on the difficulty of the items you have already answered. You can always change your response by selecting a different choice before clicking "Answer Confirm."

- Your main goal while taking the GRE exam is to respond to every question, because using this approach should have a positive effect on your score. At the same time, avoid taking a "wild guess" at any answer you are unsure of, since doing that may lower your score.

Tip #86: What to Do When Your Test Day Arrives

Since room temperatures may vary at the test center, dress

in layers. Your ID verification when you arrive may be done by thumb printing, the use of photography or videotape, or through some other method of electronic confirmation. Aside from that, personal digital assistants (PDAs), cell phones, Blackberrys, and other personal items cannot be brought into the testing area. You will be told where to deposit them for safekeeping until you are ready to leave the test center. This is what you should expect:

1. **When you arrive at the test center.** If you have an authorization voucher from ETS, it will be required of you at that time, along with a handwritten confidentiality statement and names of business schools where your test scores should be sent. A sign-in, sign-out process will also be in place, and scratch paper will be provided for your use during the timed portion of the test.

2. **Before the test begins.** You will be given up to 30 minutes to complete an untimed tutorial, much like an athlete warming up before an important game. After you begin the test, you will be able to click the Help link to review the directions or check the tutorial, if necessary, but every section of the test is timed. Also, because certain items are too large to appear on the screen, you will need to use the scroll bar on the right to respond to certain questions.

3. **While you are taking the test.** As you proceed, follow the directions carefully and avoid spending an undue amount of time on any individual item. You can refer to the on-screen clock display to check the time remaining for the section, and it will alert you when five minutes are left for you to complete the section. Also, as the computer

screen will indicate, a ten-minute recess will be available to you at the appropriate time.

The blank, ten-page booklet you will be given to use as "scratch paper" (along with a fine-point marker) has a faint grid pattern, which is useful for drawing math diagrams and arriving at your answer by process of elimination when that is the right approach. If you fill this booklet while working on the questions, you can raise your hand to request a replacement. These booklets, or note boards as they are sometimes called, may not be removed from the testing room, and you will be required to hand them in when the testing session is complete.

What Your GRE Test Scores Will Say About You

With the method used to calculate scores for the GRE exam, the number of correct responses is adjusted to allow for the difficulty level of the individual items contained in the test. In this calculation, your score will be based on the complexity of the questions you complete, your competence in answering them, and the total number of your responses.

To some degree, the scores applicants receive when taking the test may be interpreted differently, depending on the graduate school where they plan to enroll. In addition to their scores, those who take the GRE receive a percentile rank for their performance, indicating their scholastic standing as it relates to the larger group being tested. Applicants are penalized for any questions left unanswered, and the results are sent to the related graduate school's admissions office ten to fifteen days after completion and scoring of the test.

How Your GRE Exam Will Be Scored

This series of standardized, multiple-choice tests measures the verbal and quantitative reasoning, analytical writing, and critical-thinking skills the student has developed up to that point. The verbal and mathematical portions of the examination are scored on a scale from 200 to 800. The analytical writing score is recorded on a 0 to 6 scale, with half-point increments. Since the quantitative and verbal sections of the GRE are adaptive, the questions given will adjust to your level of performance as you go through the test.

The Choices You Will Have After Completing the Test

When you complete the exam, you will have the option of canceling your scores, and this cancellation will apply to every section of the GRE. If you decide to do this, neither you nor any educational institution will receive your scores, and it will be as if you had never taken the test at all. You may repeat the test if you think your scores are not true indicators of your scholastic ability, but be aware that a large score increase in a second attempt at the exam is rare, and your scores may go down if you take the test again.

Your Unofficial and Official GRE Test Scores

Immediately after completing your test, you will be able to view your unofficial scores for the verbal and quantitative sections, excluding the Analytical Writing Assessment (AWA), which is graded differently. Your official score report, which will also include your AWA results and is covered by your registration fee, will be sent to you and your designated score recipients within ten to fifteen days after you have taken the GRE.

Your GRE scores will be retained for five years, and all scores that you earn during that period will be sent to your designated score recipients as you choose, but you may not request to have only those scores from a particular test date submitted if you have taken the exam more than once.

Using the GRE Basic Diagnostic Service

Those who have taken the general test within the past six months and received their official score report may use this free service for information related to every question contained in the verbal and quantitative sections of the GRE, including the exact skill being tested, the difficulty level of the question and its type, whether they answered the question correctly, and the amount of time they took to answer the question.

Using the Question-and-Answer Review Service for the GRE Exam

For a fee of $50, you can go over the verbal and quantitative questions that you answered incorrectly on the GRE and compare your responses to the correct answers. These sessions will be conducted approximately 30 days after you complete the GRE and for up to 60 days after that.

Taking a Test in Your Specialty Along with the GRE Exam

If your score on GMAT test for admission to business school is more than 40 points below that particular school's average score, that may prove to be a negative factor when you apply, and a high score would be in your favor when it comes to admission. The specialty exam is a tool that graduate schools can use as a basis for comparing students with diverse academic backgrounds who apply for admission, along with their GRE results, and the other components that make up the application.

A Broader View of What You Will Need to Get Through Graduate School

While scoring well on the GRE and GMAT exams is important, there are many other skills that individuals need to succeed in business school and beyond — including motivation, relevant work experience, leadership potential, and good social skills — and students' interviews and admissions essays are also important factors. Applicants should contact the graduate schools that interest them and determine how they use these test scores and other criteria, including letters of recommendation and the grades students earned while working toward their undergraduate degree, in making a decision related to admission.

For more information regarding the admissions process for graduate school business programs and related careers for those who already have an MBA degree, you can visit **www.mba.com**.

Conclusion

Business schools consider the GRE exam an indicator of an applicant's future academic success, along with the GMAT. Since you will want to do your best on test day, steps you can take to ensure a favorable outcome include:

- Become familiar with the test components.

- Prepare for the GRE by using books, practice tests, and special software.

- Know how to register for the GRE and what you should do on test day.

- Know how the test is scored and what those scores mean.

CHAPTER 11
HOW THE GMAT EXAM WILL FIT INTO YOUR PLAN

The GMAT, which will be your specialty test for business school, is made up of four sections, and like the GRE exam, those sections are timed separately. It is also a CAT, but only basic computer skills are required, including typing your essays and choosing your answers to the multiple-choice questions. The related test centers offer students the solitude and privacy of individual work stations, and there are two scheduled breaks during the exam. In addition, the top-rated business schools have confidence in this test's standards because it is administered in the same way to everyone who takes it.

Rules That Apply to Taking the GMAT Exam

Because the test is standardized, the requirements that relate to it are inflexible and no exceptions can be made, which will assure you that results of your test will be valid. When you register for the GMAT exam, and again on test day, you will be asked to agree to all applicable terms and conditions before proceeding. Since the GMAT test is meant to assess your basic verbal, mathematical, and analytical writing skills, you will not be tested on your business knowledge and skills, your area of concentration as an undergraduate, any related subject area, or your intangible qualities.

How This Test Differs from Other Graduate School Entrance Exams

The people seated around you at the test center will not be taking a test exactly like yours because of the way in which questions are presented to each applicant. Only one question will appear at a time on your screen, and you cannot skip any questions or go back to change any of your answers. While you may study typical GMAT test questions organized by type while you are preparing for the test, when you take the exam, the items it contains will not be grouped in such a precise manner.

While more than 200,000 individuals take the GMAT test annually, fewer than 50 of them achieve a perfect score of 800. This means that you should not waste valuable time while taking the test in an attempt to estimate the difficulty of the questions being presented to you or your test scores at the expense of concentrating on your responses to them.

The Questions on the GMAT

Every multiple-choice item contained in the exam has been scrutinized by professional test developers, and new ones are included whenever the GMAT test is administered. The GMAT is intended to evaluate the skills and abilities you have acquired over several years in a general way, and it will also serve as an overall indicator of your ability to succeed in an MBA program.

The Types of Questions on the GMAT

To ensure that the test material is acceptable and of high quality, the authorities who develop the GMAT test rely heavily on established standardized procedures. All items found in the exam are reviewed independently, and they are eliminated or updated whenever the need arises.

The multiple-choice questions in the quantitative section involve data sufficiency and problem solving to test your skills in arithmetic, basic algebra, and basic geometry. The verbal section will test your ability to read and understand written material, your reasoning skills, and your ability to conform to the principles of standard written English.

How to Register for the GMAT Exam

You can register for the test by telephone (call 1-800-717-GMAT) or online at **www.mba.com**. When you do, you will be given a list of test dates and times, along with the testing centers located in your area. The usual fee for registering is $250, which is payable by check, credit card, or debit card.

Tip #87: Consider the Typical Business School Applicant and the GMAT

This individual will tend to select the answer that seems to be correct for each of the test questions, with the following results:

- If the question is relatively easy, the applicant will be likely to choose the correct answer.

- For problems of medium difficulty, which receive the most attention from applicants during the test, an "educated guess" will only be correct part of the time.

- If the question is difficult, the applicant's response is almost always incorrect.

On this basis, if you take practice tests before going for the GMAT exam, you will be able to determine your current scoring level and find out if you will be spending most of your time answering questions in the easy, medium, or difficult category on test day. This will enable you to adjust your expectations accordingly.

What to Do Before, During, and After the GMAT

When you are preparing to take the GMAT test, practice identifying sentence modifiers until you can accomplish it without struggling, and you will discover they are easy to correct on test day. In addition, if you find a dangling modifier in the example you are given, look for a response that will change the meaning of the sentence and correct it.

Tip #88: Looking for Errors as You Complete the Test

When you are taking the test, follow these steps for finding and correcting the errors you discover in the examples you are given:

- Be sure to read the sentence carefully and ask yourself if anything seems to be incorrect. If you find no errors, use the choices you are given to see what concepts are being tested, determine if the original sentence is the "right" choice, and work systematically from there.

- While you must know how to detect errors, you must also know how to correct those errors by finding the right response.

- Look for the most concise answer that also is grammatically correct. In other words, avoid unnecessary wordiness, which is often present when to verb to be is used in a sentence, and eliminate that choice whenever you can.

- The use of passive voice is allowed in the test, and you should only eliminate such an item when you are given an alternative in the active voice that also is grammatically correct.

- Since the words "it" or "they" must always refer to a particular noun, proceed with caution if you see either word used as an underlined item in the test. If any pronoun is used in a sentence and there is no noun that it refers to, the use of that pronoun must be corrected.

- When you are interpreting the meaning of a sentence, you will need to know how commas and semicolons should be used to avoid confusion and misinterpretation.

- Do not overlook any of the choices you are given

in the test. Although the original sentence may not contain a grammatical error, you may also find one of the options you are given states the basic concept presented to you more clearly.

- Some choices may distort the meaning of the original sentence, even though they may be grammatically correct when taken out of context.

- To determine if the original sentence provided is the correct choice, you must be able to eliminate four of the answer choices. Rushing will increase the probability of overlooking something essential and selecting the wrong answer.

- Take note of the difference between the perfect tense, which describes a recent event or one that began in the past and is ongoing today, and the past perfect tense, which describes an event completed in the past. For example, "She has been waiting for the results since Tuesday" versus "She had been waiting for the results, but they came yesterday."

- Do not try to correct any portion of the sentence that is not underlined. Even if you feel you can improve on the wording as it stands, that is not what you are being asked to do, and you will be sidetracked if you try to do it.

- When you are dealing with comparisons, do not add or take out any items, and make sure the two parts of the comparison match grammatically.

- When dealing with a complicated sentence, begin with what you are sure of, eliminate the choices that you feel are incorrect, and focus on the concepts that fall into the gray area of uncertainty.

- Try to spend no more than a minute and a half on each question in this section because of the prevailing time constraints.

Part One of the GMAT — Completing the AWA Section

While you are writing the two essays required in this section, you may be surprised to discover you will not be given a choice of topics. You may also be interested to know that business schools requested this section, thus giving verbal skills the importance they deserve. In addition to your score for the AWA, the schools to which you apply will receive a copy of your essays. Since the readers who grade them take a holistic approach to your essays, their quality will be assessed on their overall impact, rather than on any minor details you may have included.

The Purpose of the AWA Section

This section is intended to measure your skill in thinking clearly and communicating your ideas to others. You will start by completing two 30-minute AWA essay questions. The next two sections, quantitative and verbal, are allotted 75 minutes each, and they contain multiple-choice items. When you begin the test, you will find yourself answering questions that are moderately difficult. Those that follow will be adjusted to your skill level by the system, depending on whether your responses are correct. This is the reason those seated around you will not be taking the same test.

Any form of plagiarism when you are completing the AWA is unacceptable, and test administrators will cancel your test scores if it is detected in your essays. Here are some pertinent details:

1. **What the essay section is like** — When writing your essays, which should be at least four paragraphs long, you will use a simple word-processing program. This means you will be free to use the functions you need — undo, redo, copy, cut, and paste — without difficulty. These essay topics fall into two categories: analysis of an issue and analysis of an argument; you will be asked to write one essay in each category.

2. **Essay One (analyzing an issue).** In the first essay, you will be asked to analyze an issue or opinion and then indicate your point of view on that topic. To accomplish this, you must state your reasons or use examples to support your point of view, based on your experience, your past reading, or your observations. In this case, using one or two carefully considered examples will be more effective than a lengthier list that is not well thought out. Also, you will only be rated on your skill in writing analytically — think carefully before taking a stand on the issue under discussion.

As you write, try to use the English language effectively. Correct usage includes sentence variety, correct grammar, and a good vocabulary. In addition, when you analyze an argument in your second essay, you will be expected to show your basic knowledge of the principles of logic, which you may want to review before taking the exam.

3. **Essay Two (analyzing an argument)**. In the second essay, you will be asked to write a critique of the argument that is presented to you, rather than give your opinion, as you did in Essay One. Any examples you provide should be well developed, you can discuss any alternative explanations that may apply, and your response ought to read like a complete narrative rather than a skeletal outline.

Handling Experimental Questions Throughout the GMAT Exam

You may be surprised to know that approximately one-fourth of the questions on your test (nine of the thirty-seven quantitative questions and eleven of the forty-one verbal items) are experimental, and they will not count toward your score. Also, earlier questions in the section count more than later ones. Since any answer you leave blank will automatically lower your score, leaving a question unanswered should be avoided. While you should not guess at an answer to a question, you should try to narrow down your choices. You will find that the scrap paper you are given at the test center is ideal for this.

Tip #89: How This Adaptive Test Will Be Scored

When you begin the GMAT exam, the computer system will start to determine what will become your final score. Each question is worth a certain number of points, and if you answer incorrectly during the early stage of the test, you will be given an easier, less valuable question to answer. In addition, an incorrect response will mean the score will be reduced by 10 or 20 points, along with the skill level of several questions that follow.

Conversely, if you answer correctly at this point, you will be given a more difficult, more valuable question as your next item. With this in mind, it is best to work slowly and carefully at the start and then pick up the pace as you get into the rhythm of the test, which will enable you to finish within the allotted time and respond effectively.

Part Two of the GMAT Exam — Mathematical Testing

Some of the items in this section will be regular problem-solving questions that will seem familiar to you because of previous tests you have taken, such as the Scholastic Assessment Test (SAT) or GRE exam. Interspersed within these items are data sufficiency questions that will ask you to decide if you can provide an answer based solely on the information you are given.

There are no questions related to trigonometry, calculus, or advanced geometry in the test, but surprisingly, your skill in business-type math, which you studied as an undergraduate, will not be tested either. Instead, you will only be tested on your knowledge of basic arithmetic, elementary algebra, and the key concepts of geometry in this portion of the GMAT.

The Purpose of the Mathematical Testing Section

These questions are intended to test your skill in analyzing the problem you are given, determining which information provided in the question is pertinent, and deciding when you have enough data to solve the problem. In this section, your goal will be to classify every example according to the fixed answer choices listed, rather than working out a solution on your own. These are some of the skills that will be tested:

1. **Answering the data sufficiency questions found in the test.** Each question in this category contains introductory information followed by statements (1) and (2), and your choices will be as follows:

   - Statement (1) can stand alone but statement (2) cannot.

   - Statement (2) can stand alone but statement (1) cannot.

   - Either statement can stand alone.

   - A combination of both statements provides the answer.

   - A combination of both statements does not provide the answer.

2. **Answering the basic geometry questions found in the test.** These questions tend to combine two or more concepts in the same problem, and this is the reason you will find it helpful to visualize certain lengths and areas that must be measured as parts of larger lengths and areas whose measurements are already known. In addition, you should focus on the diagrams provided as the source of information you need to answer a particular question.

3. **Using the "back-solving" method as you work.** If you use this process, you can work out the answer to a question by trying the various choices you are given until you are

satisfied. This means you should begin by taking one of those choices and relating it to the question. If that choice does not fit, you can move on to one of the others until you find the answer that fits the question. If the choices provided involve variables, try to begin with the last option and work up to the others. If the choices have concrete values, begin with the middle value and go on from there. The back-solving approach will be especially helpful when solving an algebraic equation.

4. **Handling word problems in this section.** When dealing with word problems, you will want to make a diagram to aid you in visualizing the question, and you should read the concept that each term represents carefully. You should also be familiar with the formulas used for calculating time, rate, and distance. The mixture problems found in the test often involve percents that require you to use this formula: *Part = Percent X Whole.*

The first problem you are asked to solve will be of medium difficulty, and you will then be presented with another problem that is more or less difficult, based on the correctness of your initial answer. Once you have solved three or four of these items, the system will estimate your potential score level, and the 33 questions that follow will determine your exact score for the mathematical section.

5. **Arriving at your answer in this section.** As you work on solving a problem, focus on each statement by itself initially, and then evaluate the statements as a unit if none of them seems to be complete. In answering the question after reading it carefully, avoid any false assumptions based on the figures you see, since they may not be drawn to scale.

These questions will ask you to solve the problem presented and select the best of the five choices listed. You should read the question carefully, consider the information you are given, and determine exactly what is being asked. If the problem seems complicated and you cannot determine the answer quickly, you should only spend about two minutes on each item. You may decide to choose the response that seems to be correct because of the timing of this section.

In other words, there may be times while taking the GMAT test that making an educated guess will be your only option, and whether your answer is correct, it will be an indication of your skill level. The questions that follow will be adjusted accordingly. Throughout this section, try to work at an even pace, check the on-screen clock from time to time, and note that you will be given an erasable notepad for working out problems when no figure or diagram is included.

Part Three of the GMAT Exam — Verbal Testing

This section of the test is intended to assess your skill in reading and comprehending written passages, reasoning, evaluating arguments, and correcting errors in sentences according to the rules of standard English grammar. This is the approach you should take:

1. **Correcting sentences in this section.** Here, you will be asked to detect a grammatical error in the example and then provide the correct answer from the multiple-choice responses you are given. These questions will be interspersed throughout the section, representing about a third of the items, which total 41. In this case, you are asked to select the

"best" response, which may not be the one that seems most familiar to you, especially if you are used to hearing, and perhaps even reading, English that is less formal than the text used in the test and that is also technically incorrect.

2. **Preparing for this section.** Good examples of standard written English may be found in reputable magazines and newspapers, in nonfiction books, and in the collections of essays many professors use in their writing courses. Be aware that these questions are intended to test the basic rules of English grammar, rather than some obscure fine point on which authorities may disagree. In addition, arriving at the correct answer may be more difficult than you anticipate because the sentences contained in the GMAT exam tend to be long and cumbersome. You should not make a quick, automatic response based solely on which of the choices given to you seems to "sound right."

3. **The skills being emphasized in this section.** These questions focus on two significant categories of proficiency in the English language that you will be expected to display as a graduate student and in a managerial position. This proficiency involves your ability to recognize:

- Expression in a sentence that is correct — This type of sentence is structured properly and is also grammatically correct.

- Expression in a sentence that is effective — This type of sentence transmits an idea clearly and concisely in addition to being grammatically correct and structurally sound.

4. **What you can expect as you complete this section.** You will be presented with a statement containing underlined words and asked to choose which of the multiple-choice items best expresses the idea or relationship highlighted. Since it is sometimes easier to rule out the incorrect answers in a multiple-choice question than to pick out the correct response at once, you may be able to determine the answer by process of elimination.

You should not be concerned with correcting the non-underlined part of the sentence, even if it seems to be poorly phrased. Once you have made your selection, read it back into the sentence, because you can only determine if it is correct by placing it in that context. In addition, you should consider the meanings contained in the various parts of the sentence and then combine them to determine the complete thought the sentence expresses.

5. **The skills being tested in this section** — As you complete this set of questions, your skills will be tested in the following areas:

   - **The use of basic English grammar.** In this section, you will be expected to recognize errors that violate one of the following rules and thus hinder communication and understanding on the part of the listener or reader:

   - **Noun-verb agreement in a sentence** — In a sentence, a singular subject requires a singular verb and a plural subject requires a plural verb. Also, singular nouns call for singular pronouns, plural nouns call for plural pronouns, and a pronoun is used incorrectly if the noun it refers to is unclear or nonexistent in the sentence.

- **The use of passive voice versus active voice** — When passive voice is used, the subject is the receiver of the action (verb) and the sentence is not grammatically incorrect. Passive voice is always preferred when it would be inappropriate or impossible to name the subject who is performing the action. On this basis, you should only reject passive voice when you are also given a grammatically correct choice in the active voice, which will read more smoothly.

- **The grammatical construction of a sentence** — Look for complete sentences as you go through this section. The use of sentence fragments, or incomplete sentences, is always incorrect. Your first task here will be to correct grammatical errors; any flaws in expression you may find are secondary. In other words, the option you choose does not need to be perfect to be acceptable.

As you read, take note of unnecessary wordiness, which often involves the verb "to be," and eliminate such a choice whenever you can. Also, while you will not be specifically tested on your skill in punctuation, you should know how commas and semicolons are used to arrive at your answer.

- **Parallel construction in a sentence.** When this form is used, the various elements in the sentence should balance each other. For example, "I studied hard, paced myself during the test, and earned a good score." Such a parallel is made by listing a series of things and contrasting or comparing them. Your task will be to recognize the elements contained in a parallel and see if they are all structured in the same way. In addition, the shortest answer will not always be the right one.

Parallel constructions are often indicated by pairs of words, including *between ... and* and *fewer ... than*, and if the underlined portion seems unclear, use the non-underlined portion to determine what is lacking in the parallel. Also, the subject can come after the verb in a sentence, especially when expressions such as there is or there are are used. You will only be able to choose the correct answer safely if you have eliminated the other four options for reasons that are specific and valid. If you work with conditional sentences, or when varied verb tenses are used within a sentence, take note of the tenses and decide if they are being used correctly.

- **Modifying phrases in a sentence.** Once the related error is detected, it is not difficult to correct. These phrases are often set off by commas, and they provide additional information related to the subject or object in the main clause of the sentence. Because they are often misplaced and commonly misused in everyday language, both oral and written, they are one of the most challenging elements you will find in this section. To handle them with ease on test day, try your hand at identifying them in books, newspapers, and magazines you read as part of your preparation for the GMAT exam.

- **Using idioms in a sentence.** These are forms of speech found in everyday language that seem to follow no general rules or pattern and that cannot be interpreted literally. You need to recognize the idiom being used in the sentence and decide which of the options sounds best, based on your experience. In addition, make certain the terms related to quantities are idiomatic in form. When the choices you are given include a verb followed by various prepositions, you will need to find the idiom by determining which preposition is correct, given the context of the related sentence.

6. **Critical-reasoning questions in the GMAT exam.** Approximately 11 questions in the verbal section fall into this category, and they involve reading short passages of about 20 to 100 words. The typical passage consists of an argument and attempts to convince the reader that the argument is a valid one. In the passage, pieces of evidence are provided, assumptions are made, and a conclusion is reached.

The Purpose of Critical-Reasoning Questions in the GMAT

This section is intended to measure your skill in argument construction and evaluation, along with plan development and evaluation, but you will not be expected to have any previous knowledge of any topic being discussed in a particular passage that you read. Your task here will be to read your answer choices so carefully that you can detect the slightest inaccuracy.

The incorrect choices found in this section will include one that suggests the complete opposite of what the passage you read maintains, a choice beyond the scope of the passage, and a definite distortion of the facts. In this context, the word "some" can mean "one or more," and most of us are unfamiliar with this broad definition of the word.

Tip #90: How to Handle the Critical-Reasoning Questions

When you are dealing with critical-reasoning questions, which test your ability to think clearly, note that every single word counts, since the passages are brief and their meaning is exact. Follow these steps as you respond to them:

- **Read the *question* before you read the *passage.*** Initially, you may feel you will be working in reverse order if you do this, but taking that step will help you determine whether you are expected to undermine an argument being presented or determine the best conclusion for it.

- **Look for the evidence, assumptions, and conclusion that form the basis of the question presented to you.** An assumption is an unstated but necessary part of an argument, and it is used in forming a conclusion. If the removal or denial of a statement means the argument carries no weight, this is a clear indication that the statement must be assumed to support the argument. Look for the scope of the argument from the start, and eliminate any irrelevant choices you are given.

To avoid being sidetracked by the fine points and language of a particular question, which will cause you to lose time, concentrate on the meaning behind it to determine what is being said. In this case, the evidence is made up of the reason a certain conclusion is reached, and the assumptions are the other points needed to back up the conclusion. You also should avoid selecting answer choices in inference questions that seem to intensify the argument being presented rather than clarify it.

- **Become familiar with the common concepts being tested in this section.** To dissect a difficult question, try interpreting the item in simpler language until it seems perfectly clear to you, and proceed from there. The basic logical patterns found in this section of test questions are consistent, although factors such as names, places, and events will vary. In addition, an argument may be based on the concept that a certain action should be taken; whether it can be done is not a concern here.

Anyone taking the test ought to be aware of details provided in the question, but there is no reason to try memorizing them or to understand all of them completely, unless they relate directly to what is being asked. You will also need the ability to visualize situations presented to you from various viewpoints, and you must be able to draw your conclusion from several levels.

- **Determine when alternative explanations are needed.** Here, the proposed argument is weak because the evidence can lead to more than one conclusion, or the conclusion may have more than one cause. In other words, the argument is incomplete. This is the kind of thing we often point out to others in our day-to-day conversations by asking, "What is your point?"

6. **Learn how to handle difficult critical-reasoning questions** —Four main types of questions found in this category are assumption, weaken-the-argument, strengthen-the-argument, and causation, and they can be further divided into the following groups:

- **Numbers and statistics questions.** You often will be asked to interpret the statistics provided to reach a conclusion. In this section, concentrate on percentages and ratios, because you will be tested on your ability to distinguish between raw numbers and ratios. You will also want to avoid reading more into the data than what is there.

When you are dealing with this type of question, you may need to work on some examples to make certain you fully understand a particular numerical concept used in the text.

- **Surveys and studies questions.** Approach these questions, which may also include experiments, cautiously, because you may need to understand how the results reported in such cases can be misinterpreted, leading to a false conclusion, or be asked to determine if some component of the project makes the results invalid. You will also want to consider whether the results provided truly represent the opinions of the entire survey group.

- **Scope-shift questions.** Here you will find a subtle shift in emphasis, such as referring to "top managers" at one point in the argument and "all managers" in another to justify the conclusion being made through faulty argumentation. To answer these questions, you need to determine what is being used as evidence and what makes up the conclusion, and then decide if those two factors are the same. If they are not, that means a shift in emphasis of some kind has taken place, no matter how subtle it may be.

- **Causation questions.** In this case, the danger lies in false reasoning in which the result is mistaken for the cause; for example, stating only one factor created a particular problem when several others were also involved. To find the answer, you will need to recognize causation in all the various ways it will be suggested to you by the wording of the passage and understand how to determine whether a statement is consistent with the facts as they are stated in the example.

- **Alternative explanation questions.** Here, the proposed argument is weak because the evidence can lead to more than one conclusion, or the conclusion may have more than one cause. In other words, with this type of question, a problem exists because the argument presented to you is incomplete.

- **Explain-a-paradox questions.** In this case, you will be asked to find a reasonable explanation for something that, at first glance, seems to present a paradox that cannot be reconciled. The trick is to rephrase the case as a question and select the choice that provides a valid solution to your query, making sure the answer completely satisfies you and can stand on its own without any assumptions on your part. In addition, the information you are given remains true, and while you can reconcile that information, you will not be able to change it.

- **"Odd man out" questions.** With these items, you will be asked to select the response that does not meet certain criteria. As you read the question, look for structural signals that shed light on the author's intent in writing the item. Words like "however" and "but" indicate a contrast of some kind, and you should pay particular attention to whatever follows. Also, your ability to rephrase the choices you are given will be important in choosing your answer.

When you are answering such a question, look for clues related to whatever category applies to the passage you are reading, go over it carefully, and then begin ruling out your choices by process of elimination. Also, as you prepare for the GMAT, learn to recognize the difference between causation and correlation, because the exam has many ways of testing applicants on making this distinction.

Section Four — Reading Comprehension Questions in the GMAT Exam

You may find this the most familiar section when taking the test, and reading comprehension is considered essential in business and in many other fields. The questions will be interspersed throughout the section, representing about a third of the 41 total items. Each passage appears on the left side of the screen, while the questions appear on the right. This format will enable you to refer back to the passage if necessary as you determine your answer. Here are a few things to consider:

1. **What you can expect as you complete this section.** The passages you read are used to assess your ability to comprehend, analyze, and apply the facts and ideas you find in the passage provided, and your response should be based solely on what you read. Reading comprehension questions are meant to be a challenge. Here, it is best to concentrate on key words and phrases so that you can see what is being asked and use the information you are given to arrive at the answer.

The test makers who compile the GMAT exam aim to provide correct answers that show respect for professional people and the United States, and they hesitate to use passages that imply strong emotion, although moderate emotion is acceptable. Today, the test also contains a diversity passage related to a marginalized group in American society, such as African Americans or Latinos, and any answer choice that expresses a negative opinion regarding one of these groups is almost certainly incorrect.

The Purpose of Reading Comprehension Questions in the GMAT

There are six categories of questions in this section, and they are intended to test your skill in the following areas:

- Finding the main idea contained in the passage you have read.

- Finding the supporting ideas in the passage and distinguishing them from the main idea.

- Finding the inferences, or ideas implied by the author that are not stated explicitly, in the passage.

- Applying the information contained in the passage to another context.

- Analyzing and evaluating the organization and logic of the passage. In this case, you will be asked to understand what you read and evaluate the passage.

- Determining the style and tone used by the author by considering the passage as a whole and focusing on that person's choice of words.

2. **Additional suggestions for answering reading comprehension questions.** As you go through the test, do the following when you read each passage:

   - Try to find the author's main idea and determine why he or she wrote the piece without being sidetracked by details. Paraphrase the text to apply the information found in the passage. The goal is to determine the message contained in the passages, which range from 200 to 350 words in length, and retrieve the information you need to answer each question correctly.

   - The topic of the particular passage you are reading will be related to the humanities, the social sciences, the biological or physical sciences, or business-related issues. The last-named group may also include human resource management, economics, or marketing items.

   - Outline each passage as you read to determine what

the author is trying to say. Since the GMAT test is computerized, you can take notes while you are reading to improve your comprehension and answer the questions more easily. In addition, the items in this section will cover only a small fraction of the information contained in the passage.

- The test is timed, and you will not want to become bogged down in any one question. To avoid this, try to devote four minutes or less to reading a passage and a minute or so to answering each question that goes with it. Also, each question should be answered solely on the basis of what is stated or implied in the passage you are reading.

- When a general question is asked, you will have to select the main idea it contains, and you may also need to know its structure. If you are given a specific question that relates to a detail contained in the passage, you may need to read it a second time to arrive at your answer.

- Look for the structural signposts that will lead you to the main idea contained in the passage. For example, the item you are reading may state that many people have found a way to free themselves of their particular addiction by following a "twelve-step program" to recovery. In addition, certain trigger words, including but and however, indicate a shift in emphasis in the text; other words, including similarly and likewise, are a sign the author is continuing the same train of thought with no change in emphasis.

- Sentences and sentence fragments found within parentheses may contain information you are looking for. They should not be regarded as secondary or unimportant when compared to the remainder of the text.

3. **Handling reading comprehension questions by category.** Use the following suggestions as you complete various types of question found in this section:

   - **Answering the social science questions.** With this category, your goal will be to apply what you learn from the passage to other topics to arrive at the correct answer. Certain statements, known as "strengtheners" and "weakeners," which are also found in the critical-reasoning section, reinforce or detract from the assumptions made by the author elsewhere in the text. In the case of passages that mention a number of theories or theorists, note that you are being tested on your ability to keep elements you find in the passage in order, and they should be given priority as you determine your answer.

   - **Answering the general science questions.** In this case, you will need to dissect the passage until you discover the author's main area of concern and reason for writing it, and can paraphrase them into the simplest terms possible. Beware of responses that attempt to link two or more elements found in different parts of the passage, and note that you may not find the author's complete main idea until you finish reading it.

You should also pay particular attention to comparisons found in the choices you are given to determine whether they are valid. You do not want to become bogged down in the details contained in the passage, unless the question makes that a necessity. As an aid in doing this, you may want to jot down a "road map" with the key information found in the text to remind yourself about where the supporting data can be found. This will be especially useful when responding to what are known as "primary purpose" or "main idea" questions. Also, the incorrect answer choices may use the same terminology found in the passage, and you will need to concentrate on the overall meaning of those responses to find the right one.

Conclusion

Like the GRE, this specialty test, which is computer-adaptive, is made up of four sections. To get the results you are looking for, do the following:

- Know the rules that apply to taking the GMAT exam.

- Become familiar with the test components and learn how to respond to them.

CHAPTER 12
PREPARING TO TAKE THE GMAT EXAM

The people who write this test think in predictable ways, and the questions it contains follow certain patterns as well. With this in mind, and to score well on the test, as you prepare for it, you should try to think like the test makers. Educators believe most applicants spend their time answering questions at their level of ability correctly or questions that are a bit more difficult incorrectly. This means that preparing for the GMAT exam should enable you to answer more questions in the second category correctly and thus increase your score. However, you will not be able to see your score or the process used to keep track of your progress as you go through the test.

Tip #91: What Your Plan of Action Should Be as You Get Ready for the GMAT

To familiarize yourself with the format of the test, you can visit **http://www.mba.com** and download the free *GMATPrep®* software designed specifically to assist you in getting ready for the exam. You should be ready to study diligently for the test, and your preparation should take a minimum of four weeks. In addition, this is the time to go over the sample multiple-choice questions available for related sections of the test and read the background articles provided.

This software includes two full-length, timed, computer-adaptive tests, and the delivery simulates what you will be dealing with on test day. It also contains a set of practice questions for every category found in the actual test, the matching answers, and a comprehensive math review. Also, real-time scoring of all multiple-choice sections of the exam is included, and you will be able to track your progress.

For additional sample test questions to review, you can purchase the *Official Guide for GMAT® Verbal Review and the Official Guide for GMAT® Quantitative Review* on their Web site.

Tip #92: How to Develop Your Individual Studying Strategy

As the framework of the GMAT verifies, every business school applicant is unique, but there are also a few recognized methods of learning that apply to everyone. You should identify your learning style, if you have not already done so, follow the steps recommended for a given category, and proceed from there as you get ready for test day and the courses that follow:

1. **Study suggestions for audial learners.** If your sense of hearing is dominant in helping you learn new things, the vast amount of reading assigned to you in graduate school may become a problem at times, but you can take certain steps to turn this potential liability into an asset:

- Try taping your classes to capture important details you may not have been able to include in your notes.

- Arrange to have another classmate, relative, or friend as a study partner. When you work together, you should review whatever topics were covered during class, analyze the material, and discuss the points that seem relevant.

2. **Study suggestions for visual learners.** If you tend to learn this way, you may take copious notes and sometimes fail to absorb key points discussed in class unless you write them down and make them your own. You may also be easily bored or have difficulty when a conversation becomes too lengthy or complicated. You can compensate for this tendency if you do the following:

   - Read the assigned material thoroughly and take careful notes of what you have read.

   - Write a brief paragraph, summarizing the information presented, and clarify it for yourself if you are studying a complex topic.

3. **Study suggestions for manual learners.** The term "hands-on experience" has a wider application than you may realize at first, and you can work with this tendency, both in and out of graduate school, by taking these steps:

   - Spend some observation time in a facility that relates to your business-related field of interest. This may include accounting, advertising, banking, business administration, public administration, business law, healthcare, human resources, nonprofit management, project management, marketing, small business, consulting, or e-commerce.

- Try to obtain an internship or do some related volunteer work to provide the practical, real-world experience you need to complement the knowledge you will gain through your coursework.

Few of us fit precisely into one of the categories mentioned previously, although you may determine one tendency seems to dominate in your case and have developed some good study habits over the years related to it. Your aim here should be to do a little experimenting and determine what study method will work best for you in business school.

Developing Your Professional Writing Style to Prepare for the GMAT and Your Future Career

Anything written that falls into this category, including e-mail, is meant to convey certain information to the reader or to request information from that person. With this in mind, you should aim for accuracy, completeness, and conciseness whenever you compose any document. The key here is to organize your material well, consider the audience you want to reach with your message, and then write for that target group or individual. After that, you can proofread what you have written to catch any grammatical errors or misspellings and make any editorial changes or additions you feel are needed.

Tip #93: Preparing for the Essay Portion of the GMAT

The AWA section of the GMAT is an important part of the test, and you should practice writing essays based on the complete list of essay topics found at the Web site to be ready for test day. As you write your practice essays, take the following steps to get the greatest benefit from them:

- **Make the structure of your essays your first concern.** Ideally, they will contain an introductory paragraph, two to three related paragraphs, and your conclusion. Also, while the issue topics often have political implications, you should not become bogged down in your own opinions or reveal anything too personal in nature, since this is neither the time nor the place for that.

- **Try to use transitional phrases as you write to make your meaning clear.** Terms such as "therefore," "consequently," and "because" will help the computer system and fellow human beings who read your essay identify certain concepts found within and between the paragraphs more easily.

Tip #94: Improving Your Reading Comprehension for the GMAT

To prepare for this section of the GMAT and the vast amount of formal, academic reading you will be doing for your courses in business school, you should develop a professional outlook toward any reading that your studies or your position in the workplace will require. It will help you get the most out of any GMAT prep courses you may decide to take. Here are some suggestions to increase your skill in reading comprehension:

1. **Do not skip the preface when you begin to read a book.** The preface contains basic information you will need to understand the author's perspective and purpose in writing it, the book's format, what makes the text unique, and the author's background and expertise. This will all lay the foundation for comprehending what you will read in the chapters that follow.

2. **Read the introduction to the text as a guide.** The introduction provides an overview of what is to come and contains background information that you will need to get the most out of the book and the course you are taking.

3. **Try using the SQ3R (Survey, Question, Read, Recite, Review) Method to improve your reading comprehension.** The following steps should prove an effective way of bringing this skill up to the professional level a manager is expected to achieve:

   - **Survey the material you are reading.** Begin by taking a look at the topic headings to get an overview of what you are reading, skim the text, and read the final paragraph to determine the author's main message. Doing this will help you adjust to the reading and become comfortable with it, even if the text is obscure.

   - **Question the material while you are reading.**

After looking at the headings in the chapter you are reading, use them to form questions that will be answered to your satisfaction as you read. Doing this will help you focus your attention on what you need to learn from reading the text.

- **Read the material to find answers to your questions.** As you read each section, try to answer the question you formed when you were surveying the text. If you are unable to do it, you will need to reread the text until you fully comprehend it.

- **Recite the answer to your question once you have found it.** As you read each section, look away from the text and try to verbalize the answer to the question you have posed in your own words. Every time you succeed, this will tell you that you understand the material you have just covered. When you are unable to do it, read the section once again and try to answer the question once more before moving on.

- **Take the time to review what you have read.** Once you have completed the entire assignment, go over the questions and answers you have developed and look over your notes as well. This will help you determine how the assignment fits in with your overall studies and with the related course in particular, what makes it significant, and how it can be applied. You also should consider any questions that remain unanswered.

4. **Reread the material when it becomes necessary.** This

is often required when we are trying to master difficult concepts as we study. Even if you do not adopt the SQ3R Method, look over the table of contents, preface, headings, and subheadings that highlight the text. Besides relating to the author's intent, think about your instructor's purpose in assigning this particular text as part of the course.

5. **Take notes as you read.** Using whatever method works for you, make brief notes that summarize what you are reading to focus on the essentials contained in the text, and prepare any questions for your instructor related to the material.

Making Online Preparation for the GMAT Exam a Priority

Since this test is a unique, computer-adaptive test, you should spend at least 50 hours online preparing for it, if only to master its format and boost your self-confidence. Also, online prep courses will be convenient to take, since you can adapt them to your schedule, and much of their content can be downloaded directly from the Internet or sent to you via e-mail as an attachment.

Tip #95: How You Will Benefit from Taking This Step

Highlighting your preparation for the GMAT by working online will also solve the following problems for you before test day arrives:

- **Exercising your eyes to prepare for the test.** Since

you will be spending nearly four hours in front of a computer screen on test day, the ideal way to get ready for this experience is by testing yourself on your own computer at home.

- **Mastering all of the material covered by the test.** The GMAT encompasses a vast amount of content, and a good online course will display hyperlinks to other sources that offer a variety of solid content in the exact areas you need to review.

- **Practicing the wide range of skill levels that will be tested.** The GMAT is an individualized test that can be enhanced by disciplined and individualized preparation. A reliable online course provides this, combined with 24-hour online tutor support.

- **Having your practice essays evaluated.** In an online course, you will be able to complete practice essays under timed conditions. The Web site **www.800score. com** offers a service that will allow you to submit essays for evaluation and receive constructive feedback on them to sharpen your professional writing skills.

Taking Classes to Prepare for the GMAT Exam

While this method of preparation may be more expensive and your schedule for preparation time may not be as flexible as it would be with online instruction, it will also provide definite support and motivation to be ready for test day. Many students find this method useful in helping them determine where their weak spots are. One top-of-the-line preparation course, for example, includes 1,400 pages of pertinent material, 25 hours of telephone tutoring support, 42 hours of class instruction, and 15 practice tests.

Tip # 96: Finding the GMAT Preparation Classes That Are Right for You

To select a prep course that will make the investment of your time and money worthwhile, the following steps are recommended:

- **Enroll in courses offered by business school-affiliated instructors.** As a rule, they will have the greatest insight into what admissions officers expect of their applicants, what it takes to be a successful manager, and what the demands of the modern business world are.

- **Try to attend an MBA fair in your area.** While you may spend time talking to business school graduates and admissions officers, you will also have an opportunity to discuss your concerns with representatives of the test-preparation companies or attend the GMAT presentations that are part of the program. Those who organize such an event will choose only reputable companies as participants, and you can match information you accumulate with your particular needs to make your plans complete.

If you want to make the most of the professional fairs you attend — either at this point in your life or later on in your career

— it will require a bit more effort than taking some résumés, business cards, and reference lists with you and showing up at the appointed time, which is a half-hearted effort at best.

To motivate yourself and show others that you are serious about finding the right business school or the right job, take the following steps when attending a career fair:

1. **Find out who the participants will be.** Ordinarily, the companies being represented at such an event are listed at the appropriate Web site or in the brochures and other materials used to promote it, including newspaper advertisements. This means that, once again, you can use your research skills to find out whatever you can about the companies on the list that interest you, with special emphasis on their hiring needs and financial status.

2. **Prepare for the career fair as you would for a job interview.** Try going through a "mock interview" with a friend or family member so that you can practice the typical questions most job hunters are faced with. In addition, compile a list of questions you want to ask about an organization in order to determine if you would want to work there, and dress professionally.

3. **Be proactive once you are at the event.** Speak to the representatives from the companies that interest you, explain why you would like to work for that company, and indicate what you feel you have to offer them. In addition, answer their questions unhesitatingly, include your own questions, and ask for additional information, such as the admissions officer or company representative's business card or a brochure about the organization or business school.

4. **Do some follow-up work after the career fair.** Making use of the material you collected, send letters to the admissions officers or company representatives on your list, thanking them for meeting with you and telling them that you will be calling in a day or two as a follow-up. This step is just as important as any preparation you might make *before* you attend the event.

The Advantages of Taking GMAT Test Prep Classes

The cost of this training must be viewed in perspective, because your earning power should increase significantly once you have earned your MBA. If maintaining a flexible schedule is your goal as you prepare for the exam, note that some of the most highly regarded companies offer weekend prep courses that will help you succeed and save time and money. In addition, once you decide to take such a course, your instructor will guide you in developing the right study habits in any weak areas you may have, give you the self-confidence you need, and keep you from getting discouraged about taking the test.

Tip # 97: Participating in a Study Group to Prepare for the GMAT

Taking part in a study group will help you develop your skill in working with a team, and it will also facilitate the completion of class projects and homework assignments once your courses begin and will serve as an aid in your test preparation. Since you want to find a study group that is right for you, here are some tips you can use to ensure that the study group you organize or join will carry out the purpose for which it was intended and that you benefit from being part of it:

- Make certain the group is of a reasonable size. If it is too small, the group may not be helpful to individual participants; if it is too large, the meetings will seem like additional class sessions.

- Choose people who are genuinely interested in participating and who have something to contribute to the group.

- Select one person to conduct the group's meetings or have the participants take turns doing this.

- Establish a schedule for your sessions that is convenient for everyone, and determine the starting and stopping times.

- Keep the group focused by following an agenda at each meeting, as many organizations do.

Tip #98: Recommended Books You Can Use for GMAT Preparation

You may also find these publications helpful as you get ready to take the test:

- *Cracking the GMAT®* from The Princeton Review, Inc., New York, NY, 2007. Related Princeton Review texts include Cracking the GMAT, *Cracking the GMAT with DVD, Math Workout for the GMAT, Verbal Workout for the GMAT, Best 282 Business Schools, Business School*

Essays That Made a Difference, Math Smart for Business, and Word Smart for Business.

- *GMAT® 800 2007-2008 Edition* from Kaplan Publishing, New York, NY, 2006.

- *The Official Guide for GMAT® Quantitative Review from General Management Admission Council,* 2005. Other recommended texts include GMAT *Comprehensive Program,* GMAT *Premier Program,* GMAT *Premier Program New York Metro Edition,* GMAT *Verbal Workbook,* GRE & GMAT *Exams Math Workbook, and Get Your M.B.A. Part-Time: For the Part-Time Student with a Full-Time Life.*

- *The Official Guide for GMAT ® Review* from General Management Admission Council, 2005.

Conclusion

For the most part, your success in taking the GMAT will depend on what you do to prepare for it. This should include the following:

- Developing your individual studying strategy and individual writing style.

- Making online preparation for the GMAT a priority.

- Choosing other options that seem appropriate — taking classes, participating in a study group, or using recommended texts.

CHAPTER 13
WHAT TO EXPECT AS YOU TAKE THE GMAT EXAM

Although these two factors seem obvious, they are essential and worth emphasizing: You should make every effort to develop a positive attitude toward the test — which is most easily achieved by preparing well for it — and get sufficient rest the night before you are scheduled to take it.

Tip #99: What to Do When Your GMAT Test Day Arrives

When you leave for the test center, you will need to bring valid identification, the names of business schools where you would like your GMAT test scores sent, and a printout of the confirmation e-mail you received from Pearson VUE related to your scheduled test.

Promptness is essential on test day, because if you arrive more than 15 minutes late for your scheduled appointment, you may not be admitted at all, and your test will be forfeited.

1. **When you arrive at the test center.** To start, you will be required to present proper identification and to officially accept the *GMAT Examination Testing Rules and Agreement*. Then your fingerprint, signature, and photograph will be

taken. Be aware that audio and video recording will take place in the testing room as you complete the exam. Also, before you begin the test, you will be required to agree to the *GMAT Nondisclosure Agreement* and *Terms of Use* statement before you can continue.

2. **Following the established GMAT test procedures —** According to the regulations, PDAs, cell phones, Blackberrys, and other personal items cannot be brought into the testing area. You will be told where to deposit them for safekeeping during the test. A sign-in, sign-out process will also be in place, and scratch paper, according to your need, will be provided during the timed portion of the GMAT.

You should go to the test center alone, because it will not have a large waiting area and anyone who accompanies you will not be allowed to stay. The length of the testing period is approximately four hours, including two breaks, and you are not permitted to discuss the test content with anyone while testing is taking place, during the breaks, or when testing is completed. In addition, eating, drinking, and smoking are not allowed inside the test center.

3. **When you have completed the GMAT exam —** After you have taken the test, you will be asked to answer a set of questions covering the following topics:

   • Your demographics and background information.

   • Whether you want to receive information or participate in surveys generated by participants of the Graduate Management Admission Search Service® (GMASS®), which is free and voluntary.

Tip #100: Why the GMASS May Interest You

This service, which is available through the GMAC, promotes communication between MBA programs and potential applicants to business school. Using information provided by individuals who take the GMAT exam, the service matches them with the admissions criteria established by recognized business schools. When a "match" between a school and a potential student is made, GMASS sends the name and address of that candidate for admission to the school to be accessed by authorized admissions officers. The applicant's privacy also is assured. Here are a few things to remember:

1. **What the GMASS can do for you.** Your participation in this valuable program will enable you to widen your search for the right business school because it can introduce you to programs you might never have discovered while doing your own research.

2. **Factors business schools will consider when they receive your information.** These include your personal information, geographic location, academic background, educational objectives, and career goals.

3. **What happens when the business school feels you may be a "match" for them.** You will be contacted either by e-mail or regular mail and provided with pertinent information that you may be able to download on your computer. Regardless of the form your mail takes, you may also receive brochures, fliers, program overviews, application forms, and invitations to related on-campus events to familiarize you with the school as a whole and its MBA program in particular.

Conclusion

When the day for your GMAT exam arrives, you should know how to follow the established procedures, what happens when you complete the test, and what the GMASS can do for you.

Chapter 14
The GMAT Test Scores and What They Mean

These scores will be based on the number of your responses, whether those responses were correct or incorrect, and the level of difficulty and unique components of each item contained in the related section of the test. They will also be classified as excellent, above average, average, or below average in relation to the scores of other people who took the test at the same time.

Understandably, your GMAT test scores may cause you more anxiety than any other part of your application to graduate school. Once they are forwarded to the business schools where you have applied, the admissions officers will view them as indicators of your future success in completing the academic part or core curriculum of their program. However, since the GMAT exam is only one element in the application process, insiders tell us that not all those who earn a score of 700 on the test are admitted to every business school where they apply.

How Your GMAT Exam Will Be Scored

Your test will be evaluated on a fixed scale, and you will be given four scores — verbal section (ranging from 9 to 44), quantitative section (ranging from 7 to 50), AWA section, and total. For the first two sections, your scores will range anywhere from 0 to 60, and they are not comparable, because different skill sets are tested in each section. Also, while the total GMAT test score ranges from 200 to 800, about two-thirds of those who take the test fall into the 400 to 600 range.

In addition to these ratings, you will receive a percentile rank for each of your scores, indicating the percentage of those individuals taking the test who ranked below you, based on the entire group being tested at that time. Because of the test specifications that have been established for the GMAT, business schools can compare the test scores of their applicants, despite the fact that they have each responded to a different set of questions and, in a sense, did not take the "same" test.

Scoring the AWA Section of Your GMAT Exam

To calculate your AWA score, the analysis of an issue portion and the analysis of an argument portion will be rated separately on a scale of 0 to 6 in half-point intervals and then averaged to obtain your final score. To accomplish this, two independent ratings will be given, and one of them may be done by an automated essay-scoring system.

Why the Scoring for this Section Is Different from the Others

This score is arrived at separately from the multiple-choice items contained in the other sections of the GMAT, and it is completely separate from the verbal, quantitative, and total scores mentioned previously. In addition, if the two rankings involved in the scoring vary by more than a point, the final score is determined by an "expert reader."

The faculty members who are trained to read your AWA essays will rate them on the quality of your ideas as they relate to the essay topics, your skill in organizing, developing, and expressing those ideas with pertinent reasons and examples, and your familiarity with the standards of basic English grammar.

Understanding the AWA Scoring Scale

The scoring scale applied to this section when the two required essays are rated may be interpreted as follows:

- **Outstanding.** This Level 6 AWA component contains an outstanding assessment of the material presented, combined with writing that is masterful and effective.

- **Strong.** This Level 5 AWA component contains a thorough assessment of the material presented, combined with credible, effective writing.

- **Adequate.** This Level 4 AWA component contains an acceptable assessment of the material presented, combined with acceptable effective writing.

- **Limited.** This Level 3 AWA component may possess characteristics similar to Level 4, but it is also somewhat flawed.

- **Seriously flawed.** This Level 2 AWA component contains serious weaknesses throughout.

- **Fundamentally deficient.** This Level 1 AWA component does not measure up to any acceptable standards.

Using the AWA Rescoring Service

If you feel your scores for the AWA section are incorrect, you have the option of having your essays rescored, but this will not apply to your scores from the verbal or quantitative portions of the test. Also, your request will only be honored within the six-month period after you have completed the GMAT, and the results of this rescoring — which you and your designated score recipients will receive in approximately 20 days — will be considered final. To request this service, complete the Analytical Writing Assessment Rescore Request Form and submit it to the GMAT Customer Service Department.

Not All GMAT Test Score Results Are Created Equal

A number of business schools consider certain sections of the GMAT test more significant than others, indicating there is a certain correlation between the quantitative score and essential MBA courses that are part of their core curriculum. If the school you select follows this practice, they may have minimum requirements related to the total score, minimum requirements related to certain sections of the test, or both.

How Business Schools You Apply to Will Interpret Your Test Scores

GMAC has established guidelines for interpreting GMAT test

scores, which are provided to all graduate schools that are designated to receive them. Since each admissions office has its own method for evaluating these scores, there is no established "passing" or "failing" grade, and, of course, they are only one part of the complete application process.

As the evaluation of your GMAT scores begins, admissions officers will consider your combined quantitative and verbal score, which is based on a 200-to-800-point scale, along with your undergraduate GPA. After that, if your combined GMAT score and GPA fail to meet the school's established standards for admission, the application process will end at that point.

If you are still in the running as the acceptance process continues, the school will then consider your GMAT analytical writing score. If you have a high score in that section (5 or 6), the admissions officer may overlook your low GMAT verbal score, but this is a rare exception that you should not rely on.

Understanding Your Unofficial and Official GMAT Test Scores

Immediately after completing your test, you will be able to print out your unofficial scores for every portion, excluding the AWA section, along with the total score. Your Official Score Report, which will include your AWA results and is included in your registration fee, will be sent to you and to a maximum of five designated score recipients (business schools) approximately three weeks later. You will not be able to change or delete this list once your choices have been made.

If you ask to receive this report online, you will be sent an e-mail with a link to your Official Score Report within a 20-day period following the test. You can also request that additional copies of your Official Score Report be forwarded to business schools by phone, regular mail, fax, or online for a fee.

Understanding Your Complete GMAT Test Score Report

This report from GMAC will include all of your test scores from the past five years and your most current AWA responses, along with the pertinent contact and background information you provided when registering for the test. The digital photograph you submitted at the test center will be sent with this report to the score recipients you have chosen, provided they have requested this information.

Tip #101: What to Do if You Are Dissatisfied with Your GMAT Test Scores

When you complete the test, you have the option to cancel your scores at that time, and this cancellation will apply to every section of the GMAT. If you do this, the scores cannot be reinstated, and the cancellation will be noted on your permanent record.

If you decide you want to take the test again, there is a 31-day waiting period before you can do this. Also, many graduate schools will use your best scores, rather than your most recent score, as their basis for accepting you. In addition, most applicants do not see a significant increase in their scores if they choose this option.

If you think your test scores are not true indicators of your scholastic ability and you want to be retested, you will need to devote more time to preparation or try a different approach to earn the scores you are hoping for.

Conclusion

While you may handle other parts of your business school application rather smoothly, your GMAT scores could cause you a certain amount of anxiety. To bring it down to a reasonable level, you will want to know:

- How your test will be scored.

- How the business schools that receive them will interpret those scores.

- What goes into your various score reports.

- What you can do if you are dissatisfied with those scores.

APPENDIX

GMAT Practice Questions

Problem Solving

1. A project scheduled to be carried out over a single fiscal year has a budget of \$12,600 divided into 12 equal monthly allocations. At the end of the fourth month of that fiscal year, the total amount actually spent on the project was \$4,580. By how much was the project over its budget?

(A) \$380   (B) \$540   (C) \$1,050   (D) \$1,380   (E) \$1,430

2. Substitute the value for n in each answer choice, and then simplify to determine whether that value results in an integer.

(A) $\dfrac{100+1}{1} = \dfrac{101}{1} = 101$

(B) $\dfrac{100+2}{2} = \dfrac{102}{2} = 51$

(C) $\dfrac{100+3}{3} = \dfrac{103}{3} = 34.333$

(D) $\dfrac{100+4}{4} = \dfrac{104}{4} = 26$

(E) $\dfrac{100 + 5}{5} = \dfrac{105}{5} = 21$

3. Rectangular floors X and Y have equal area. If floor X is 12 feet by 18 feet, and floor Y is 9 feet wide, what is the length of floor Y in feet?

(A) $13^{1/2}$ (B) 18   (C) $18^{3/4}$ (D) 21   (E) 24

4. A case contains c cartons. Each carton contains b boxes, and each box contains 100 paper clips. How many paper clips are contained in two cases?

(A) 100bc   (B) $\dfrac{100b}{c}$ (C) 200bc   (D) $\dfrac{200b}{c}$ (E) $\dfrac{200}{bc}$

5. The sum of prime numbers that are greater than 60 but less than 70 is

(A) 67   (B) 128   (C) 191   (D) 197   (E) 260

Data Sufficiency

In each case, you will choose from the following answers.

(A) Statement (1) *alone* is sufficient, but statement (2) *alone* in not sufficient.

(B) Statement (2) *alone* is sufficient, but statement (1) *alone* in not sufficient.

(C) Both statements *together* are sufficient, but neither statement *alone* is sufficient.

(D) Each statement *alone* is sufficient.

(E) Statements (1) and (2) together are not sufficient to answer the question asked.

6. How much is 20 percent of a certain number?

    (1) 10 percent of the number is 5.

    (2) 40 percent of twice the number is 40.

7. Is r greater than 0.27?

    (1) r is greater than $1/4$.   (2) r is equal to $3/10$.

8. What percent of a group of people are women with red hair?

    (1) Of the women in the group, 5 percent have red hair.

    (2) Of the men in the group, 10 percent have red hair.

9. In a certain class, one student is to be selected at random to read. What is the probability that a boy will read?

    (1) Two thirds of the students in the class are boys.

    (2) Ten of the students in the class are girls.

10. If n is an integer, is $n + 1$ odd?

    (1) $n + 2$ is an even integer.   (2) $n - 1$ is an odd integer.

Reading Comprehension

During the nineteenth century, occupational information about women that was provided by the United Stated census — a population count that is conducted each decade — became more detailed and precise in response to social changes. Through 1840, **simple** enumeration by household mirrored a home-based agricultural economy and hierarchical social order: the head of the household (presumed male or absent) was specified by name, whereas other household members were only indicated by the total number or persons counted in various categories, including occupational categories. Like farms, most enterprises were family-run, so that the census measured economic activity as an attribute of the entire household, rather than of individuals.

The 1850 census, partly responding to antislavery and women's rights movements, initiated the collection of specific information about each individual in a household. Not until 1870 was occupational information analyzed by gender: the census superintendent reported 1.8 million women employed outside the home in "gainful and reputable occupations." In addition, he arbitrarily attributed to each family one woman "keeping house." Overlap between the two groups was not calculated until 1890, when the rapid entry of women into the paid labor force and social issues arising from industrialization were causing women's advocates and women statisticians to press for more thorough and accurate accounting of women's occupations and wages.

11. The primary purpose of this passage is to

    (A) explain and critique methods used by early statisticians

    (B) compare and contrast a historical situation with a current-day one

    (C) describe and explain a historical change

    (D) describe historical opposition to an established institution

    (E) trace the origin of a contemporary controversy

12. Each of the following aspects of the nineteenth-century United States censuses is mentioned EXCEPT the

   (A) year in which data on occupations began to be analyzed by gender

   (B) year in which specific information began to be collected on individuals in addition to the head of the household

   (C) year in which overlap between women employed outside the home and women keeping house was first calculated

   (D) way in which the 1890 census measured women's income levels and educational background

   (E) way in which household members were counted in the 1840 census

13. It can be inferred from the passage that the 1840 United States census provided a count of which of the following?

   (A) women who worked exclusively in the home

   (B) people engaged in non-farming occupations

   (C) people engaged in social movements

   (D) women engaged in family-run businesses

   (E) men engaged in agriculture

14. The author uses the word **simple** most probably to emphasize that the

   (A) collection of census information became progressively difficult throughout the nineteen century

   (B) technology for tabulating census information was rudimentary during the first half of the nineteenth century

    (C) home-based agricultural economy of the early nineteenth century was easier to analyze than the later industrial economy

    (D) economic role of women was better defined in the early nineteenth century than in the late nineteenth century

    (E) information collected by early nineteenth century censuses was limited in its amount of detail

15. The passage suggests which about "women's advocates and women statisticians"?

    (A) They wanted to call attention to the lack of pay for women who worked in the home.

    (B) They believed that previous census information was inadequate and did not reflect economic changes in the United States.

    (C) They had begun to press for changes in census-taking methods as part of their participation in the antislavery movement.

    (D) They thought that census statistics about women would be more accurate if more women were employed as census officials.

    (E) They had conducted independent studies that disputed the official statistics provide by previous United States censuses.

Critical Reasoning

16. In order to increase profits during a long slowdown in sales, the largest manufacturers of automobiles have instituted record-setting price increases on all their models. The manufacturers believe that this strategy will succeed,

even though it is inconsistent with the normal relationship between price and demand.

The manufacturers' plan to increase profits relies on which of the following assumptions?

(A) Automobile manufacturers will, of necessity, raise prices whenever they introduce a new model.

(B) The smaller automobile manufacturers will continue to take away a large percentage of business from the largest manufacturers.

(C) The increased profit made on cars sold will more than compensate for any decline in sales caused by the price increases.

(D) New safety restraints that will soon become mandatory for all new cars will not be very costly for the manufacturers to install.

(E) low financing and extended warranties will attract many price-conscious customers.

17. "Life expectancy" is the average age at death of the entire live-born population. In the middle of the nineteenth century, life expectancy was 40 years, whereas now it is nearly 80 years. Thus, in those days, people must have been considered old at an age we now consider the prime of life.

Which of the following, if true, undermines the argument above?

(A) In the middle of the nineteenth century, the population of North America was significantly smaller than it is today.

(B) Most of the gains in life expectancy in the last 150

years have come from the reductions in the numbers of infants who die in their first year of life.

(C) Many of the people who live to an advanced age today do so only because of technology that was unknown in the nineteenth century.

(D) The proportion of people who die in their seventies is significantly smaller today than is the proportion of those who die in their eighties.

(E) More people in the middle of the nineteenth century engaged regularly in vigorous physical activity than do so today.

18. From June through August 1987, Premiere Airlines had the best on-time service of 10 United States airlines. From January through March 1988, Premiere Airlines had the worst on-time service of the 10 airlines. The on-time performance ranking of the other nine airlines relative to each other remained unchanged.

Which of the following, if true, would contribute to an explanation of the facts above?

(A) Although Premiere Airlines only revoked its policy of routinely holding flights for late passengers in the fall of 1987, the other nine airlines never had that policy.

(B) Premiere Airlines reduced its business by 10 percent when it raised its rates in the fall of 1987 to compensate for rising gasoline costs.

(C) Premiere Airlines bought five new planes in the fall of 1987 that proved to have fewer mechanical problems than the ones they replaced.

(D) Premiere Airlines serves New England, which has

heavy winter snowfalls, whereas the other airlines do most of their business in the warmer regions of the country.

(E) Although all 10 airlines strive to keep their flights on schedule, overcrowded airports increased flight delays for all 10 airlines in January 1988 as compared with June 1987.

19. Homeowners aged 40 to 50 are more likely to purchase ice cream and are more likely to purchase it in large amounts than are the members of any other demographic group. The popular belief that teenagers eat more ice cream than adults must, therefore, be false.

The argument is flawed because the author___________.

(A) fails to distinguish between purchasing and consuming

(B) does not supply information about homeowners in age groups other than 40 to 50

(C) depends on popular belief rather than on documented research findings

(D) does not specify the precise amount of ice cream purchased by any demographic group

(E) discusses ice cream rather than more nutritious and healthful foods.

20. Not all life depends on energy from sunlight. Microbial life has been found in bedrock more than five kilometers below the surface of the Earth, and bacteria have been found on the deep ocean floor feeding on hydrogen and other gases rising from the interior of the Earth through vents in the ocean floor.

The statements above, if true, best support which of the following as a conclusion?

> (A) The location in the bedrock where microbial life was found was not near a system of volcanic vents through which hydrogen and other gases rose from the interior of the Earth.

> (B) Bacteria are able to exist at the molten center of the earth.

> (C) A thorough survey of a planet's surface is insufficient to establish beyond a doubt that the planet contains no life.

> (D) Life probably exists on Sun-orbiting comets, which are cold agglomerations of space dust and frozen gases.

> (E) Finding bacterial remains in coal and oil would establish that the bacteria had been feeding on substances that had not been produced from the energy of sunlight.

Sentence Correction

Choose the answer that produces the most effective sentence and is without grammatical error.

21. Although a surge in retail sales <u>have raised hopes that there is a recovery finally</u> underway, many economists say that without a large amount of spending the recovery might not last.

> (A) have raised hopes that there is a recovery finally

> (B) raised hopes for their being a recovery finally

> (C) had raised hopes for a recovery finally being

(D) has raised hopes that a recovery is finally

(E) raised hopes for a recovery finally

22. Of the vast tides of migration that have swept through history, <u>maybe none is more concentrated</u> as the wave that brought 12 million immigrants onto American shores in little more than three decades.

   (A) maybe none is more concentrated as

   (B) it may be that none is more concentrated as

   (C) perhaps it is none that is more concentrated than

   (D) maybe it is none that was more concentrated than

   (E) perhaps none was more concentrated than

23. Diabetes, together with its serious complications, <u>ranks as the nation's leading cause of death, surpassed only</u> by hear disease and cancer.

   (A) ranks as the nation's third leading cause of death, surpassed only

   (B) rank as the nation's third leading cause of death, only surpassed

   (C) has the rank of the nation's third leading cause of death, only surpassed

   (D) are the nation's third leading causes of death, surpassed only

   (E) have been ranked as the nation's third leading causes of death, surpassed only

24. A survey by the National Council of Churches showed that in 1986 there were 20,736 female ministers, almost 9 percent of the nation's clergy, <u>twice as much as 1977</u>.

(A) twice as much as 1977

(B) twice as many as 1977

(C) double what it was in 1977

(D) double the figure for 1977

(E) a number double that of 1977's

25. As its sales of computer products have surpassed those of measuring instruments, the company has become increasingly willing to compete for market sales <u>they would in the past have conceded to rivals</u>.

   (A) they would in the past have conceded to rivals

   (B) they would have conceded previously to their rivals

   (C) that in the past would have been conceded previously to rivals

   (D) it previously would have conceded to rivals in the past

   (E) it would in the past have conceded to rivals

Answers

1. A	2. C	3. E	4. C	5. B
6. D	7. B	8. E	9. A	10. D
11. C	12. D	13. B	14. E	15. B
16. C	17. B	18. D	19. A	20. C
21. D	22. E	23. A	24. D	25. E

[1] *The Official Guide for GMAT® Review* from General Management Admission Council, 2005.

BIBLIOGRAPHY

Publications

1. *Cracking the GMAT®*, The Princeton Review, Inc., New York, NY, 2007.

2. *GMAT® 800 2007-2008 Edition*; Kaplan Publishing, New York, NY, 2006.

3. *The Official Guide for GMAT® Quantitative Review*; General Management Admission Council, 2005.

4. *The Official Guide for GMAT ® Review*; General Management Admission Council, 2005.

Web Sites

1. 5 Tips to Help You Be a Better Listener, **http://www. associatedcontent.com/article/176333/5_tips_to_help_you_ be_a_better_listener.html.**

2. 10 Things to Know About Background Checks, **http://msn. careerbuilder.com/custom/msn/careeradvice/viewarticle.as px?articleid=702&SiteId=cbmsn4702&sc_extcmp=JS_702_ advice&catid=js.**

3. 10 Tips for When You Apply for a Scholarship, **http://www. associatedcontent.com/article/388128/10_tips_for_when_you_ apply_for_a_scholarship.html.**

4. 11 Time Management Tips, **http://sbinfocanada.about.com/cs/ timemanagement/a/timemgttips.htm.**

5. 15 Ways to Leave Your Job, **http://msn.careerbuilder.com/ custom/msn/careeradvice/viewarticle.aspx?articleid=1000&Sit eId=cbmsn41000&sc_extcmp=JS_1000_advice&catid=cj.**

6. Accelerated MBA Programs/One-Year MBA, **http://www. mba360.com/accelerated-mba-programs.html.**

7. The Admissions Interview Process: What You Need to Know, **http://gradschool.about.com/cs/interviews/a/admint.htm.**

8. Advantages of Preparing for the GMAT Online, **http:// www.800score.com/mba-center.html.**

9. Advertising Management Degree Info – Masters Degree Review, **http://educhoices.org/articles/Advertising_Management_ Degree_Info_-_Master_Degree_Review.html.**

10. A Guide to Nonprofit-Focused Graduate Programs – An MBA with a Twist, **http://nonprofit.about.com/od/nonprofitwork/a/ gradschl.htm?p=1.**

11. Applying to Business School: Breathing Life into Your Application, **http://www.princetonreview.com/mba/apply/ articles/application/life.asp.**

12. Applying to Graduate School? How to Prepare an Organized Packet for Your Recommenders, **http://www.associatedcontent. com/article/278621/applying_to_graduate_school_how_ to.html.**

13. Applying to Graduate School? – Tips for a Strong Statement of Purpose, **http://www.associatedcontent.com/article/274413/ applying_to_graduate_school_tips_for.html.**

14. A Sensible Approach to Job Hunting Online, **http://msn. careerbuilder.com/custom/msn/careeradvice/viewarticle.as px?articleid=178&SiteId=cbmsn4178&sc_extcmp=JS_178_ advice&catid=js.**

15. Assess Careers and the MBA, **http://www.mba.com/mba/As- sessCareersAndTheMBA.**

16. Avoid Getting Stuck in Middle Management, **http://www. associatedcontent.com/article/100824/avoid_getting_stuck_in_ middle_management.html.**

17. The Basic Components of Effective Internet Marketing, **http:// www.associatedcontent.com/article/539183/the_basic_ components_of_effective_internet.html.**

18. Book Review — Best 290 Business Schools, **http://businessmajors. about.com/od/choosingaschool/gr/Best290schools.htm.**

19. Business Majors: Entrepreneurship, **http://businessmajors. about.com/od/specializations/a/EntBusMajors.htm.**

20. Business Plan Outline, **http://sbinfocanada.about.com/cs/ businessplans/a/bizplanoutline.htm.**

21. Business School Case Studies, **http://businessmajors.about.com/ od/casestudies/a/casestudybas.htm.**

22. Career Strategies: How to Spot a Bad Company Before You Take a Job, **http://www.associatedcontent.com/article/338932/career_ strategies_how_to_spot_a_bad.html.**

23. Check the Benefits Before Changing Jobs, **http://msn. careerbuilder.com/custom/msn/careeradvice/viewarticle.asp x?articleid=1277&SiteId=cbmsn41277&sc_extcmp=JS_1277_ advice&catid=js.**

24. Choosing an MBA Program, http://www.associatedcontent.com/article/223718/choosing_an_mba_program.html.

25. Climb the Management Ladder to Success, http://www.allbusiness.com/human-resources/employee-development-leadership/11513-1.html.

26. Computer Systems MBA, http://www.unhmba.org/mba-programs/computer-systems-mba.html.

27. Conflict Management and Negotiation Degree Information - MBA Degree Review, http://educhoices.org/articles/Conflict_Management_and_Negotiation_Degree_Information_-_MBA_Degree_Review.htm.

28. Corporate Culture, http://www.associatedcontent.com/article/181052/corporate_culture.html.

29. CPA with MBA: Extra punch or just extraneous, http://www.startheregoplaces.com/todayscpas/careeroptions/dualdegrees/?SSID=198EB0C0F6B3473FA36551D29CF69492&printView=true.

30. The Dangers of Being a Micromanager, http://www.allbusiness.com/human-resources/employee-development-leadership/11235-1.html.

31. Dealing with Difficult People, http://www.associatedcontent.com/article/7313/dealing_with_difficult_people.html?page=2.

32. Distance-Learning MBA Programs for Working Adults, http://www.mba-online-program.com/online_mba_distance_learning.html.

33. Distance-Learning Pros and Cons, http://www.quintcareers.com/distance_learning_pros-cons.html.

34. Distance-Learning Student Loans, http://oedb.org/loan/

distance-learning.

35. Effective Business Leadership and Management, http://www.associatedcontent.com/article/20274/effective_business_leadership_and_management.html.

36. Entrepreneurship MBA, http://www.unhmba.org/mba-programs/entrepreneurship-mba.html.

37. Ethics in Business, http://www.associatedcontent.com/article/42180/ethics_in_business.html.

38. Finding the Right Employee, http://www.associatedcontent.com/article/28106/finding_the_right_employee.html.

39. Find Your Program, http://www.mba.com/mba/findyourprogram.

40. Five Important Interview Tips, http://msn.careerbuilder.com/custom/msn/careeradvice/viewarticle.aspx?articleid=1252&SiteId=cbmsn41252&sc_extcmp=JS_1252_advice&catid=iv.

41. Five Reasons Why You Need a Mentor, http://msn.careerbuilder.com/custom/msn/careeradvice/viewarticle.aspx?articleid=806&SiteId=cbmsn4806&sc_extcmp=JS_806_advice&catid=wi.

42. Five Signs of Job Burnout . . . And What to Do About It, http://msn.careerbuilder.com/custom/msn/careeradvice/viewarticle.aspx?articleid=696&SiteId=cbmsn4696&sc_extcmp=JS_696_advice&catid=wl.

43. Five Ways to Get More Confidence at Work, http://msn.careerbuilder.com/custom/msn/careeradvice/viewarticle.aspx?articleid=713&SiteId=cbmsn4713&sc_extcmp=JS_713_advice&catid=wi.

44. Five Ways to Punch Up Your Cover Letter, http://msn.

careerbuilder.com/custom/msn/careeradvice/viewarticle.aspx?articleid=503&SiteId=cbmsn4503&sc_extcmp=JS_503_advice&catid=cl.

45. Getting Your Student Visa Category F-1 for Study in the USA, http://www.associatedcontent.com/article/240433/getting_your_student_visa_category.html.

46. Global Management MBA, http://www.unhmba.org/mba-programs/global-management-mba.html.

47. GMAT Essay Section Guide, http://www.800score.com/gmat-essay.html.

48. GMAT Prep and MBA Admissions Info, http://www.gmat-mba-prep.com/mba-admissions.html.

49. GMAT Test Prep, http://www.gradview.com/articles/tests/preparing_for_gmat.html.

50. GMAT Test Review, http://www.admissionsconsultants.com/gmat/index.asp.

51. The Graduate Management Admission Council, http://www.gmac.com/gmac.

52. Graduate School, http://gradschool.about.com.

53. GRE: Graduate Record Examinations, http://www.ets.org/portal/site/ets/menuitem.fab2360b1645a1de9b3a0779f1751509/?vgnextoid=b195e3b5f64f4010VgnVCM10000022f95190RCRD.

54. Healthcare Administration (MBA) Master's Degree Program, http://degreedirectory.org/articles/Health_Care_Administration_(MBA)_Master's_Degree_Program.html.

55. The Hidden Dangers of Multitasking, http://www. associatedcontent.com/article/112836/the_hidden_dangers_ of_multitasking.html.

56. How to Be a Better Manager, http://management.about.com/cs/ midcareermanager/a/htbebettermgr.htm.

57. How to Be the Best Listener You Can, http://www. associatedcontent.com/article/144559/how_to_be_the_best_ listener_you_can.html.

58. How to Complete a FAFSA, http://businessmajors.about.com/ od/payingforschool/ht/FAFSA_Form.htm?p=1.

59. How to Choose a Career Counselor, http://www. associatedcontent.com/article/352181/how_to_choose_a_ career_counselor.html.

60. How to Correct Damaging Errors on Your Credit Report, http:// www.associatedcontent.com/article/285405/how_to_correct_ damaging_errors_on_your.html.

61. How to Delegate Responsibility, http://www.associatedcontent. com/article/7305/how_to_delegate_responsibility.html.

62. How to Fill Big Shoes, http://msn.careerbuilder.com/custom/ msn/careeradvice/viewarticle.aspx?articleid=1043&SiteId=cb msn41043&sc_extcmp=JS_1043_advice&catid=wi.

63. How to Get into a Top MBA Program, http://businessmajors. about.com/od/admissions/a/GetintoMBA.htm.

64. How to Prepare Your Curriculum Vitae, http://www.aafp. org/online/en/home/publications/otherpubs/strolling/prep/ preparecv.html.

65. How to Protect Your Credit Rating, http://www.associatedcontent.

com/article/281345/how_to_protect_your_credit_rating.html.

66. How to Survive Graduate School, http://www.associatedcontent. com/article/155895/how_to_survive_graduate_school.html.

67. How to Work a Job Fair, http://msn.careerbuilder.com/custom/ msn/careeradvice/viewarticle.aspx?articleid=452&SiteId=cbm sn4452&sc_extcmp=JS_452_advice&catid=js.

68. Human Resources MBA, http://www.unhmba.org/ mba-programs/human-resource-mba.html.

69. Inside Jobs: Human Resources Executive, http://msn. careerbuilder.com/custom/msn/careeradvice/viewarticle.as px?articleid=401&SiteId=cbmsn4401&sc_extcmp=JS_401_ advice&catid=cj.

70. International Business Etiquette 101, http://msn.careerbuilder. com/custom/msn/careeradvice/viewarticle.aspx?articleid=1050 &SiteId=cbmsn41050&sc_extcmp=JS_1050_advice&catid=wi.

71. The International Classroom, http://www.gradview.com/ articles/careers/international_classroom.html.

72. Is a Career in Management Right for Me?, http://www.allbusiness. com/human-resources/careers-career-path/11583-3.html.

73. Is an International MBA for You?, http://www.princetonreview. com/mba/research/articles/find/internationalMBAs.asp.

74. Job Search Tactics: The Four "Ps" of Building a Career Presentation, http://www.associatedcontent.com/article/340419/job_search_ tactics_the_four_ps_of_building.html.

75. Keep Your Perspective: Job Interview Blunders, http://www.allbusiness.com/human-resources/ careers-job-hunting/986654-1.html.

76. Laid Off: How to Make Losing a Job a Winning Venture, http://www.allbusiness.com/human-resources/careers-changing-jobs/1620-1.html.

77. Learning to Manage Stress for Good Health, http://www.associatedcontent.com/article/250928/learning_to_mange_stress_for_good_health.html.

78. Make Your Decision, http://www.mba.com/mba/MakeYourDecision.htm.

79. Making the Transition from Military to Civilian Employment, http://msn.careerbuilder.com/custom/msn/careeradvice/viewarticle.aspx?articleid=775&SiteId=cbmsn4775&sc_extcmp=JS_775_advice&catid=js.

80. Managing a Large Staff Effectively, http://www.allbusiness.com/print/11442-1-22eeq.html.

81. Management Career Paths, http://management.about.com/cs/generalmanagement/l/blmgtpath.htm.

82. Management Skills, http://www.agmrc.org/agmrc/business/gettingstarted/businessmanagementskills.htm.

83. Master of Business Administration (MBA), Global Management Degree Overview, http://education-portal.com/articles/Master_of_Business_Administration_(MBA):_Global_Management_Degree_Overview.html.

84. Master of Business Administration: Using an MBA to Change Careers, http://www.associatedcontent.com/article/365900/master_of_business_administration_using.html.

85. The Mathematics of Persuasive Communication, http://sbinfocanada.about.com/od/smallbusinesslearning/a/bizwritingpj.htm.

86. MBA Admissions Interview, http://www.mba360.com/mba-ad-missions-interview.html.

87. MBA Degrees and Technology, http://www.mbaschools.com/technology-and-the-mba.

88. MBA FAQ, http://www.unhmba.org/mba-faq.html.

89. MBA Internships, http://www.mba360.com/mba-internships.html.

90. MBA Jobs and Job Search Strategies, http://www.mba360.com/mba-jobs.html.

91. MBA — Risk Management, http://www.mba360.com/mba-risk-management.html.

92. Minority Student Recruitment in Business School, http://www.gradview.com/articles/careers/minorities_in_business_school.html.

93. The Most Comprehensive Online Source of Graduate School Information, http://gradschools.com.

94. Nine Little-Known Ways to Advance Your Career, http://msn.careerbuilder.com/custom/msn/careeradvice/viewarticle.aspx?articleid=1256&SiteId=cbmsn41256&sc_extcmp=JS_1256_advice&catid=js.

95. Online Executive MBA Degree Programs, http://www.directdegree.com/s/ExecutiveMBA.shtml.

96. Online MBA Degree Basics, http://distancelearn.about.com/od/onlinecourses/a/OnlineMBA.htm.

97. Online MBA — E-business Specialization, http://www.worldwidelearn.com/online-mba/ebusiness-mba.htm.

98. Online MBA – Marketing Specialization, **http://www.worldwidelearn.com/online-mba/marketing-mba.htm.**

99. Operation MBA, **http://www.gmac.com/gmac/SchoolServices/OperationMBA/default.htm.**

100. Perkins Loans, **http://oedb.org/loan/perkins.**

101. Pertinent Facts About MBA Courses, **http://www.mba360.com/mba-courses.html.**

102. Prices & Fees for the GMAT Exam, **http://www.gmac.com/gmac/TheGMAT/TestTakerSupport/PricesandFees.htm.**

103. Project Management 101, **http://management.about.com/cs/projectmanagement/a/PM101.htm.**

104. The Promise of Professional Organizations, **http://www.back2college.com/professionalorganizations.htm.**

105. Relocating for Your Job: Reimbursements, Tax Deductions, Insurance Riders, and More, **http://www.associatedcontent.com/article/294129/relocating_for_your_job_reimbursements.html.**

106. Resources for Minority Applicants to B-school, **http://www.princetonreview.com/mba/apply/articles/process/resources.asp.**

107. Seven Pitfalls of Changing Jobs, **http://msn.careerbuilder.com/custom/msn/careeradvice/viewarticle.aspx?articleid=1075&SiteId=cbmsn41075&sc_extcmp=JS_1075_advice&catid=cj.**

108. Six Rules for Effective, 'Net- working, **http://msn.careerbuilder.com/custom/msn/careeradvice/viewarticle.aspx?articleid=1158&SiteId=cbmsn41158&sc_extcmp=JS_1158_advice&catid=js.**

109. Some Secrets of Effective Presentations, http://www.associatedcontent.com/article/112851/some_secrets_of_effective_presentations.html.

110. Special Reports, http://businessmajors.about.com/gi/dynamic/offsite.htm?zi=1/XJ&sdn=businessmajors&zu=http%3A%2F%2Fwww.gmattutor.com%2Freports.html.

111. Stafford Loans, http://oedb.org/loan/stafford.

112. Standardized Test Advice: An Overview of Test Day Reasoning, http://www.associatedcontent.com/article/88843/standardized_test_advice_an_overview.html.

113. Stand Out with an E-portfolio, http://msn.careerbuilder.com/custom/msn/careeradvice/viewarticle.aspx?articleid=1196&SiteId=cbmsn41196&sc_extcmp=JS_1196_advice&catid=js.

114. Study Groups — Forming a Study Group, http://businessmajors.about.com/od/studentresources/a/Study_Groups.htm.

115. Succeeding in an Online Graduate School, http://www.associatedcontent.com/pop_print.shtml?content_type=article&content_type_id=186537.

116. Succeeding in Graduate School, http://www.westmont.edu/_academics/pages/departments/psychology/pages/after_westmont/getting_in/succeeding.html.

117. Surviving a Company Merger, http://www.associatedcontent.com/article/212479/surviving_a_company_merger.html.

118. Take the GMAT, http://www.mba.com/mba/takethegmat.

119. The Teaching Assistantship: Valuable, and Paid, Experience, http://gradschool.about.com/cs/financialaid/a/teachassit.htm?p=1.

120. Ten Things to Do Today to Be a Better Manager, **http:// management.about.com/od/careerdevelopment/a/ TenThingsToDo.htm?p=1.**

121. Ten Tips on Making a Successful Career Change, **http:// www.allbusiness.com/human-resources/careers-changing- jobs/1618-1.html.**

122. Testing Accommodations for Test Takers with Disabilities, **http:// www.ets.org/portal/site/ets/menuitem.c988ba0e5dd572bada2 0bc47c3921509/?vgnextoid=ed32486227855010VgnVCM10000 022f95190RCRD&vgnextchannel=c9d7be3a864f4010VgnVC M10000022f95190RCRD.**

123. Tips for Your Graduate School Interview, **http://www. providence.edu/bio/grad/interviewP.pdf.**

124. Top 5 MBA Schools, **http://businessmajors.about.com/od/ choosingaschool/tp/topgradschools.htm.**

125. Top 5 Private MBA Loan Resources, **http://businessmajors. about.com/od/payingforschool/tp/topMBALoans.htm.**

126. Types of Financial Aid, **http://distancelearn.about.com/od/ payingforschool/a/typesofaid.htm.**

127. The Ultimate Guide to Business Majors and Programs, **http:// www.businessschools.com/majors-programs.**

128. A Very Different Degree, **http://www.princetonreview.com/ grad/research/articles/life/different.asp.**

129. Understanding the TOEFL. **http://www.princetonreview. com/testprep/testprep.asp?TPRPAGE=284&TYPE=TOEFL- ABOUT.**

130. Using a TOEFL Practice Test to Score High on the TOEFL Test,

http://www.mba360.com/toefl.html.

131. What to Expect from the Graduate Record Exam, **http://www. gradview.com/articles/tests/about_the_gre.html.**

132. Where to Find Salary Information, **http://msn.careerbuilder. com/custom/msn/careeradvice/viewarticle.aspx?articleid=927 &SiteId=cbmsn4927&sc_extcmp=JS_927_advice&catid=js.**

133. Writing for Business, **http://management.about.com/od/ communication/a/businesswriting.htm.**

134. Writing the Graduate School Application Essay, **http://www. quintcareers.com/graduate_school.html.**

135. Your GMAT Scores — What They Mean to the B-Schools and for You, **http://www.west.net/~stewart/gmat/qa_1.htm.**

136. Your First Stop for GMAT Information, **http://businessmajors. about.com/od/gmatinfo/?once=true&.**

137. Your Insider Guide to the GMAT, **http://www.gmattutor.com.**

INDEX

Made in the USA
Monee, IL
07 July 2026

56551802R00164